9-24-76

INTERNATIONAL AID
AND NATIONAL DECISIONS

Written under the auspices of the
Center of International Studies, Princeton University.
A list of other Center publications appears at the back of the book.

LEON GORDENKER

International Aid and National Decisions

Development Programs in Malawi, Tanzania, and Zambia

PRINCETON UNIVERSITY PRESS

CONTENTS

1929875

LIST OF FIGURES AND TABLES

LIST OF ABBREVIATIONS

DAS	Development Advisory Service (of IBRD)
ECA	UN Economic Commission for Africa
FAO	Food and Agriculture Organization of the UN
IBRD	International Bank for Reconstruction and Development
IDA	International Development Association
IFC	International Finance Corporation
ILO	International Labor Organization
IMF	International Monetary Fund
ITU	International Telecommunications Union
LDC	Less developed country
OPEX	Organizational, Executive and Administrative Personnel (program of UN)
Special Fund	UN Special Fund
UNESCO	UN Educational, Scientific and Cultural Organization
WFP	World Food Program
WHO	World Health Organization
World Bank	See IBRD
UDI	Unilateral Declaration of Independence by Ian Smith government in Rhodesia
UN	United Nations
UNCTAD	UN Conference on Trade and Development
UNDP	UN Development Program
UNICEF	UN Children's Fund

UNIDO	UN Industrial Development Organization
UNRRA	UN Relief and Rehabilitation Administration
UNTAB	UN Technical Assistance Board

PREFACE

The striking—indeed, explosive—growth of organized international relations during the thirty years since the end of the Second World War has been accompanied by a steady outpouring of comment, polemic, journalism, scholarly description and analysis, and theoretical construction. While this flood does not rival the tidal wave of official documentation, it could be expected to show keen sensitivity to crucial decisions and practices. Yet as I was observing international organization and directing research, I remarked a paucity of description and analysis based on close observation of the administration of the programs so grandly acclaimed in the ever more frequent international assemblies. How, students asked, and I asked myself, are those programmatic declarations, such as the United Nations Development Decade, carried out? What sort of practices and relationships develop, what are the results, and how much difference does it make in organizing international relations?

From such questions came the impetus for this study. While it derives partly from simple curiosity about the subject, it also relates to developments of real, not to say crucial, importance to the whole world. For this study deals with efforts carried on through international institutions to solve the problem of uneven economic development and to meet pressing demands from the governments of some of the least developed areas in the world for rapid change.

When this inquiry began during the mid-1960s, few scholarly writers would have predicted that within a decade most of the UN system would issue flamboyant demands for a new economic order and sharply revised relationships between poor lands and rich. In fact, most scholarship dealing with organized relationships between rich and poor countries was put together in the comfort of a high level of development. Only rarely did independent scholars go out to the field,[1] where the action eventually has to take place (if it does at all). Understandably, most worked from international headquarters, where information covering the whole world was collected and where experts could readily be consulted. Valuable as these studies are, they nevertheless suffer from a certain abstract and textureless tone. Moreover, the international secretariats in the headquarters sought not to point up failures, mistakes, and half-realized plans but to put forward favorable examples of technical assistance and preinvestment operations. Thus, abstraction developed by independent scholars was frequently complemented by self-serving specificity. No sharp notion of what the contact with international organizations meant to a government, to a ministry, to a bureau in a less developed country could be built up from such makings.

With these considerations in mind, the direction of deeper research led to national capitals, from where the actual work of international programs was supervised and frequently carried out and where such projects, at least in the first instance, were designed. From the national capitals it would be easy to find the ultimate re-

---

[1] Among the noteworthy exceptions are Walter R. Sharp, *Field Administration in the United Nations System* (New York: Frederick A. Praeger, 1961), Andrew Shonfield, *The Attack on World Poverty* (New York: Vintage, 1962), and Ronald Nairn, *International Aid to Thailand: The New Colonialism?* (New Haven: Yale University Press, 1966).

cipients of international aid—the villages, the national parks, the land settlement schemes, and the lowest echelons in the national administrations. Furthermore, in the national capitals, the process of mutual influence among national governments and international agencies —the principal issue with which this study is concerned —would be most visible. Accordingly, I decided to follow up the questions aroused by study and teaching with close field observation. Such observation must necessarily have a limited geographical scope, for international assistance programs had reached such proportions by the mid-1960s that a comprehensive field study would have required an army of researchers and a budget wildly beyond the resources of scholarship.

Yet the need to limit the field of observation accorded well with my personal predilection to depend primarily on direct surveillance and face-to-face interviews, supplemented by and based on documentary and archival materials. Such an approach, it seemed, would produce vivid detail that would counter the abstraction of general studies based on headquarters data. At the very least, descriptions of some field operations would become available. The basis of these descriptions could be found, to begin with, in the stated intentions of governments and the international agencies and also in the broader doctrines, if any, which underlay the joint programs. Furthermore, such study need not adopt one or another theoretical framework, e.g., functionalism, in an effort to verify it or some other set of hypotheses. Rather, given the intention of using a field perspective, some suggestions about previous theoretical notions might come forward without requiring the creation or revision of a general theoretical approach. From the beginning it was assumed that this study would not provide a broad enough basis for such a general construction.

While the guidelines were being defined, sheer good fortune made it possible to select interesting sites for observation. In the course of a trip to Africa on behalf of the Parvin Fellows Program at Princeton University, I found both old friends from my service in the UN Secretariat and a warm welcome from them and from national governmental officials for my thoughts about observing the work of the UN system at the field level. This conjunction of favorable auspices led to selection of Malawi, Tanzania, and Zambia as the location of my field work.

The choice had its disadvantages and its virtues. These three countries are quite different in level of development and experience from some other recipients of aid, e.g., Guatemala or India. They are small in population, generally lacking influence in international politics, and distant from the threshold of an industrial economy. In the mid-1960s they were new countries, with limited civil services which still employed colonial officials. Yet it would not have been easy to find representative developing countries. What would they in fact represent, aside from themselves? To postulate representative categories would have been a step backward toward the initial abstractions that I was keen to avoid. Malawi, Tanzania, and Zambia after all differed from each other and because they were at the beginning of their national experience offered both access to leading persons and a critical moment in their existence. In retrospect, I believe that the choice had a useful outcome, even if it led to much caution about generalizing for the whole universe of international aid on the basis of three cases.

The actual field surveys included gathering information on every field project in each research location. A full list of work underway was available, and as many as possible of the international personnel associated with each project were interviewed. Whenever possible, the actual working location was visited, so that, for example, I saw planning advisers at work in Malawi, a productivity center in Tanzania, and the fisheries advisory project on Kariba Lake in Zambia. Whenever possible, interviews were conducted with counterpart personnel and relevant officials in national ministries. From the considerable number of projects with which I became acquainted, those analyzed in this study were selected on the basis of: 1) visible operations and results, either positive or negative; 2) attention given them by international agencies; 3) visibility of relevant planning and negotiation; and 4) a presumed possibility of influence on governmental policies. While such criteria can be stated only in qualitative terms, merely setting them forth suggested which among the possible cases might best be treated in some detail.

In all three countries, the Resident Representatives of the UN Development Program generously helped my research by providing access to documents outlining the initiation and progress of the projects under their jurisdiction. They spoke frankly of their difficulties and spent many hours in discussion with me. Their documents, comments, and offices were indispensable for my investigations. Furthermore, the officials on their staffs gave me similar cooperation. The material gathered through interviews and documents in the offices of the Resident Representatives provided a firm basis for understanding key aspects of the operations in the three countries.

Similarly, generous cooperation was available from officials of all three governments, although I was unable to consult archival material with the same thoroughness made possible at UN facilities. Yet, because of my access to governmental communications in the UN files, I concluded that probably not a great deal of the content of the written record was missed. The UN offices also made it possible for me to sit in on many meetings between international officials and their national opposite numbers. I was thus able to observe at firsthand the way in which proposals and ideas became official requests.

Interviews in the field were supplemented with interviews at the headquarters of the UN Economic Commission for Africa, the Food and Agriculture Organization, the International Labor Organization, the World Health Organization, the UN Educational, Scientific and Cultural Organization, and the International Bank for Reconstruction and Development. Field officials of these organizations were also interviewed.

More than one hundred interviews were preserved in notes. Others appeared to have too little significance for formal notes, or only in a casual way confirmed material gathered elsewhere. Interviews were conducted around the following main questions: How important are the international programs in shaping development? Why? What effect do they have on governmental plans and administration? What feedback to international organizations takes place? How? What difficulties arise in planning and execution? Why? What are the sources of ideas and guidelines for international programs? To what extent do recommendations from international agencies at any level bear on what the government does? These questions were put, as far as possible, to each person interviewed. The interviewees were encouraged to expand their answers, to illustrate them with specific instances, and to discuss the political settings of their remarks. It was not my practice to take notes during the interviews but to summarize them as soon as possible afterward. Each interviewee was asked to recommend persons who could be of help. The interviews were conducted mainly between 1966 and 1968, during visits lasting from one to four weeks in each location and repeated at least once during the research period. A visit in 1970 provided an opportunity for at least some follow-up interviews. Given the rate of turnover of both national and international personnel, it must be considered fortunate that even that small number of interviews could be repeated.

The rather long period of time that has elapsed between my first visits to the three countries of observation and the appearance of this study has been one of great change in East and Central Africa. National doctrines have changed and developed, as the example of Tanzania makes so clear, and national politicians and civil servants have also moved in various ways and their ranks filled out as young people finished their training. The politico-security situation also has changed as Rhodesia can no longer depend on shelter from Portuguese colonies and as South Africa conducts a more supple foreign policy. In the world of international organizations, the impact of the Jackson Report on the capacity of the UN system is still being digested, and the World Bank has moved aggressively to expand its usefulness to the less developed countries. Thus, this study is not one of actuality, although I believe that the central issues of relationships between member governments and international institutions remain largely unchanged. Meanwhile, the passage of time, which dampens personal and official sensitivities, allows me to write with frankness.

L.G.

March 1976

ACKNOWLEDGMENTS

The basic financial support for this study consisted of a generous grant from the Social Science Research Council, supplemented by help from the Committee on Research in the Humanities and Social Sciences of Princeton University. The work was at all times a part of the program of the Center of International Studies of Princeton University, which aided in numerous ways, not the least of which was efficient typing and related services. The Rockefeller Foundation and Princeton University made possible a year at Makerere University in Uganda, where in happier times than the present I was able to deepen my acquaintance with African international politics and from where I embarked on the last series of interviews for the study. An early first draft was revised during a splendid leave year at the Netherlands Institute for Advanced Study in Wassenaar.

Each person who granted me an interview contributed in a way that deserves grateful acknowledgment here, but I must content myself with thanking them only in this general way. I do want, however, to note the special help given me by several international officials, including George Ivan Smith, Gertrude McKitterrick, A. L. Adu, Richard Symonds, Anthony Gilpin, Andrew Joseph, Kouros Satrap, and Gordon Menzies.

At various stages the manuscript was read by Peter Baehr, Martin Doornbos, and Donald McNemar, who were good enough to make useful comments and to give me encouragement. Some parts of the study also were the subject of helpful advice from some of those interviewed.

ACKNOWLEDGMENTS

Macmillan & Co. permitted the use of material in Chapter II which appeared earlier in Robert W. Cox, *International Organization: World Politics* (London: Macmillan, 1969).

To all who helped, whether named here or not, goes my gratitude, while I bear the responsibility for any faults in this work.

L.G.

INTERNATIONAL AID
AND NATIONAL DECISIONS

1.

INTERNATIONAL ORGANIZATION
AND FIELD OPERATIONS

THE constant, even frenetic, operation of several hundred international institutions of diverse models has so seeped into international relations that it is both taken for granted and regarded as an essential element by national governments. Even though few persons anywhere, and these sometimes reluctantly, pay much attention to this ceaseless, beneficially intended activity, it nevertheless concerns the general welfare and relates with special intensity to the poorer parts of the world.

Promotion of the general welfare—the provision of varied services to the people of the world—in one way or another now preoccupies most of the personnel and takes the lion's share of the finances of most of the broad membership intergovernmental organizations.[1] Although

[1] No single, up-to-date, comprehensive description of these programs can be found, but must be pieced together from official documents. Among the recent treatments of parts of this official material, together comprising the best available description, see Lester B. Pearson, *Partners in Development* (New York: Praeger, 1969), and United Nations, *A Study of the Capacity of the United Nations Development System*, UN Doc. DP/5, 1969 (Geneva: United Nations, 1969), hereafter referred to as the Jackson Report for its author, Sir Robert Jackson. See also Robert W. Cox and Harold K. Jacobson, *The Anatomy of Influence* (New Haven: Yale University Press, 1973), for comments and some description.

3

this activity has unexpectedly burgeoned, it nevertheless links with older ideas about the functions of international organizations. In fact, the general welfare
services derive for the most part from organizations
cast in a rather conventional mold, familiar to all concerned with relations among states since the creation of
the League of Nations.

Such international institutions represent attempts to
bind their members, the states of the world, to conduct
some of their affairs in regular, specified ways. These
legally binding commitments shape the expectations
that each government has about the behavior of others.
Thus a universal standard for judging the behavior and
intentions of governments is built up. Constructing
standards requires implicit or explicit specification of
desirable behavior and interpretations of rules so that
governments can guide themselves. The institutions em-
body and develop processes intended to generate the
consent of governments to new or improved policies
which will be generally executed. Some of these policies
are intended to promote the general welfare and belong
to a yet broader, perpetual pressure toward international cooperation. International institutions radiate a general hope, too often forlorn but never abandoned for
the long term, of helping to organize the mutual affairs
of governments so as to prevent war, adjust conflict, and
approach international governing.

This conventional perspective on international organization does not exclude field operations, which are a
part of this study, but neither does it necessarily include
them. It could be argued that attention to the general
welfare, including economic development and social
change, creates conditions necessary for organizing co-

4

operative, problem-solving behavior among governments.[2] If field operations are necessary to the promotion of the general welfare, then they are a positive step toward effective international cooperation.

Another perspective is offered by the Functionalist approach to international organization, which emphasizes practical, down-to-earth cooperation.[3] Symbolic commitment to standards has little place in this view, but field operations fit it perfectly. In a sense, the development of field operations by international organizations bridges the differences that have developed among those who think of relations among governments as having a primarily negotiating and bargaining character and those who would abandon such approaches in favor of concrete, directly perceptible benefits.

Both of these perspectives have a global, supragovernmental tone or even bias. Another perspective more closely approaches that of the national capitals. It shows the complex of international organizations and their hedgerows of intertwining recommendations and programs in a different light. The goals of general welfare and orderly relationships remain the same. But the deliberative organs offer the national governments a vast series of opportunities to attempt to manipulate the international structures for their own benefit, however

[2] This argument is implicit in Article 55 of the UN Charter, where "the creation of stability and well-being which are necessary for peaceful and friendly relations among nations" is connected with "higher standards of living . . . and conditions of economic and social progress and development."

[3] Perhaps the most profound discussion of functionalism is in Ernst Haas, *Beyond the Nation State* (Stanford: Stanford University Press, 1964). See also Cox and Jacobson, *Anatomy of Influence*, 33–34, 425, 431–33.

that is interpreted. Yet from this perspective, membership in international organizations has its costs; pressures on a government grow out of such participation and issues are raised, sometimes on the symbolic level, sometimes very practically, to which a government must respond.

Manipulative efforts directed outward by national governments into international bodies are extremely well-documented. Even quite casual readers of daily newspapers can learn about, for example, Egypt's attempt to use the United Nations to secure withdrawal of Israel from captured territories. Furthermore, some manipulation has an almost comforting parliamentary tone, whatever the outcome, for the unmistakable votes of majorities and minorities are registered. The influence exercised by the United States in wide-membership international bodies during the first decade after the Second World War is one illustration of this manipulation. Another can be found in the ability of the Afro-Asian nations to move the General Assembly to ever stronger resolutions to counter the policy of apartheid in South Africa. Again, the UN Conference on Trade and Development (UNCTAD) and the UN Industrial Development Organization (UNIDO) were created primarily to serve the interests of poor countries.

If manipulative attempts, especially at the symbolic level, can be treated as easily recognizable, the reaction of governments to efforts of international organizations to set behavioral patterns through recommendations, urgings, demands, and rewards is far less well understood. Because much of this reactive process necessarily takes place within and around government bureaucracies, it easily becomes and remains obscure. Moreover,

6

it necessarily differs from government to government, depending upon organizational forms and practices, political leaders and their views, and a host of other particular factors. Yet an obvious purpose for the existence of international organizations, whatever the perspective from which they are viewed, is precisely to induce reactions from member governments. Reactions of governments which result from stimulation by the activity of international organizations may be seen as the exercise of influence by those organizations.

This study relates to the generalized flow of influence from international institutions to and from member governments, but it can cover only part of the entire range of such influence. It deals with a subject matter typical of world institutions which reflect in varied proportions all of the perspectives discussed here. These are institutions which can solemnly declare a Second Development Decade after a first one scarcely triumphed in reaching for its goals. These are also institutions which can create a far-reaching administrative network and finance budgets of hundreds of millions of dollars for assistance to national economic development programs. The study centers on the manner in which international organizations work with member governments in efforts to improve the general welfare. In particular, it deals with those specialized programs that have a distinctly novel character in the development of international institutions; these are programs that depend on field operations that reach directly into member countries. Such operations have become characteristic of international institutions which are directed by their members to attempt to provide services for economic development and social change.

7

The study of influence in any social framework has long been the subject of criticism which monotonously points out the vagueness of the concept, the difficulties in making it operational for research, and the problems in measuring it. It is admittedly difficult to specify when influence, in the sense of inducing a reaction that otherwise might not have taken place, has been exercised. But this is a difficulty that applies frequently to inquiry into any kind of social phenomena: they are complex, frequently obscure, and often involve activity directed to different ends by the engaged parties. Yet it is obvious that international institutions are intended to have relations that cause behavioral reactions in governments. It is just as obvious that the causal impetus may range in intensity from the mildest sort of implied suggestion through various kinds of rewards to direct, forceful coercion. In matters of the general welfare, the causal impetus involves perceived self-interest on the part of governments (including their engaged component parts, e.g., specialized bureaucracies) and rewards for engaging in specific activities which supposedly accord with that self-interest. In this sense, the aim of international institutions is to influence governmental behavior. Evidence of such influence may be found in the manner in which governments and their personnel react to recommendations and policies emanating from international institutions and to possibilities for achieving direct benefits in programmatic form. Such reactions are commonplace in governmental circles. Furthermore, it is conceivable that some programs offered or actually operated by international institutions cause governments to react by attempting to influence the nature of the programs themselves. They may attempt to manipulate the international institutions, i.e., to influence

8

them. It is with such varieties of influence, in concrete instances, that this study is concerned.[4]

The Inquiry

From highly tentative overtures a quarter of a century ago to more intense activity to promote the general welfare, the international community appears to have defined a largely new mode of cooperation—field operations mounted by international institutions of global scope. Because of its novelty, its growth, its potential, and its limitations, it is worth asking how this mode works. This study will attempt to provide some description of recent operations in a framework restricted enough so that considerable and perhaps vivid detail can be presented.

Second, the inquiry will seek to determine what, if any, explicit ideas guide contemporary activities in the field. Much of the output of the deliberative organs of international organizations consists of urging member governments to follow one course in preference to another: thus, the United Nations urges member governments not to lose sight of the social consequences of economic change; and governments are urged to remain aware of social effects in preference to treating them with indifference. It might be assumed that personnel furnished by the UN system for field work would be guided by such recommendations and that governments would be enlightened by them. But is there evidence of such doctrinal penetration? What conclusions can be drawn from such evidence?

[4] Comments by Cox and Jacobson, *ibid.*, 3–4, are relevant here. My use of the concept appears to be consonant with theirs but differs in emphasis.

Third, if field administrative structures are created in member countries by the international organizations to which they belong, it could be expected that their operations would give a distinct tone to the policies of the recipient governments. This hypothesis will be tested as far as possible.

Fourth, if international organizations create administrative apparatus that works in different countries, it could be expected that the mode of operation is similar in each location. This hypothesis will be tested in three countries. An attempt will be made to account for any differences that occur.

Finally, some focal points of activity provide better possibilities for observation than would be found in simply broad description. One of these points is the office of Resident Representative.[5] It is hypothesized that the Resident Representative develops a crucial relationship with the host government and that he sets a distinctive mode of operation which shapes the pattern of influence.

EXTENSION OF INFLUENTIAL RELATIONSHIPS

An end product of the sprawling network of international organizations and a principal object of their programs comprises services for governments on their own territories. This obviously contrasts with the earlier pattern of centralized services, such as statistical collations, which governments were free to use as general resources. Among the services now provided are technical

---

[5] He has recently been restyled as Country Director. I will use the older title which applied during the observation period of this study.

10

advice, training, high level administrative personnel, and loans.[6] One way or another, closely or distantly, these services are intended to relate to economic development and concomitant social change deliberately promoted by recipient governments.

Because economic development is the very stuff of politics—the kernel of crucial decisions—in many less developed countries (LDCs) the work of international organizations necessarily and increasingly touches on controversial and delicate national issues.[7] To make

[6] These services are offered in various quantities and forms by different agencies of the UN system. Loans may be granted by the International Bank for Reconstruction and Development (IBRD) and the International Monetary Fund (IMF), but the latter offers only short-term loans for adjustments of foreign exchange problems. Both offer technical assistance and training, as do all of the other agencies in the UN system. Technical assistance includes advice on technical problems, demonstrations, and medium-term applied research and creation of training facilities. The two latter forms are intended to pave the way for capital investments, perhaps by the IBRD, and are the speciality of the UN Development Program (UNDP), which uses the services of the other agencies. UNDP also is a principal source of technical assistance. Training includes fellowships for study abroad, training in internationally assisted local institutions, and on-the-job training as counterpart personnel for technical assistance experts. High level administrative personnel are provided by the United Nations under the OPEX program (operational, executive, and administrative personnel).

The Jackson Report contains much description and detail on these programs. See also Pearson, *Partners in Development,* and Uner Kirdar, *The Structure of United Nations Economic Aid to Underdeveloped Countries* (The Hague: Martinus Nijhoff, 1966).

[7] "Economic development often creates new tensions and gives rise to organized interest groups which make explicit demands on government and party; it may also encourage new

11

recommendations about the organization of an educational system, to arm a minister of transport with arguments for extending a road network that competes for capital funds with a weapons-seeking defense ministry, to urge population control on a people who for the first time in the memory of the oldest man enjoy reasonably good health is to become involved in politics. True, the involvement is not partisan in the sense of taking part in an election, or as definite as would be the formal and real power to make final, authoritative, general decisions. Furthermore, formally and, so far, ultimately, the recipient government retains all powers of final decision on joint ventures and has complete freedom to accept or reject advice or loans.

Yet it is a fact—one that is characteristic of international institutions one third of a century after the formation of the United Nations—that in a large number of countries, governmental decisions for the first time in history take into account advice proffered by personnel formally representing neither private interests nor the government for whose benefit they work. These officials, employed by international organizations, operate within or (more frequently) parallel to national civil services and have access to the full range of technical working papers pertaining to the issues in their purview. Some of them take up only highly defined problems, such as the rate of flow of water in a river at various seasons over a number of years, and produce characteristically specialized reports. But some of the advisers have mandates broad enough to match such titles as

---

definitions of tribal identity and thus increase social cleavage." Henry Bienen, *Tanzania: Party Transformation and Economic Development* (Princeton: Princeton University Press, 1967), 13.

"Economic Adviser to the Government" and have direct and frequent access to responsible ministers at the top of government.

Furthermore, governments increasingly seek advisers, sometimes at the suggestion of international organization representatives, for the purpose of preparing a request for assistance on a larger scale or for a loan from one of the international financial organizations. It is ever more common to find a team of experts, sent by the UN Development Program (UNDP) or a regional UN economic commission, hard at work on plans for a training institute or a pilot plant. The counsel offered by such advisers, it might be assumed, necessarily strives to meet the standards believed appropriate for the organization from which future aid is to be sought. In this sense, a government receives outside advice in order to build into its own information and decision-making structures the standards of outside organizations. Such incorporation of international standards may take place in a scarcely conscious manner or may be quite deliberate and explicit. This line of reasoning leads to the proposition that, by seeking and receiving aid from international organizations, governments of LDCs introduce substantive advice and advisory personnel which influence their own domestic political processes. In fact, this manifestation of international organization penetrates deeper into the domestic process than was expected or earlier experienced.

A corollary of this proposition holds that the conceptions of sovereignty enshrined in the constitutional instruments of international organizations—and perhaps most strikingly in the case of the United Nations—do not precisely conform to the reality of operational programs. The time-honored principle that each government absolutely controls its policies with regard to other governments permeates these constitutional instruments, and probably also the conceptions of international cooperation held by many diplomatic personnel. In the formal, legal sense, the members of international organizations are states equal to one another in legal capacity. All have reserved domestic jurisdictions which, if the concept has any meaning, are capable of definition.

The reality of the second half of the twentieth century is that economic and social programs may have steadily eroded the margins of de facto domestic jurisdiction. Governments have progressively become involved in a process which tends to require conformity to implicit and explicit standards set in central institutions outside of their control. These standards apply to both donor and recipient countries. Donor countries may heavily influence the nature of the standards as a return for their largesse, but in doing so, they establish expectations within their own ranks and outside as to their future behavior. To deny these expectations also exacts a price. The recipient governments honor these standards in order to receive the support they need for their domestic programs. It would be inaccurate, however, to suppose that this erosion of the domestic jurisdiction has become the equivalent of control by international organizations. Far from it. But the process operated through international organizations nevertheless has an influential effect, varying from situation to situation, on their members.

This stark formulation of the decline of the private preserves of governments within their national boundaries appears to fly in the face of much honored doctrine in the LDCs. Most of these countries only recently were colonies, governed by expatriate civil servants. Others hold the memory of colonial times as a symbolic referent for judging present behavior. According to some prevalent doctrine, characteristically prominent in Zambia and Tanzania, independent statehood means the ability to make decisions by a process that in principle eschews all outside influences. Such a process insures freedom from "imperialism" and "colonialism" and constitutes a working version of the legal concept of sovereignty.

"Imperialism" and "neocolonialism" have been used so often as sweeping pejoratives that it is difficult to find agreement on what they mean. Nevertheless, their use always emphasizes the desirability of independent decision-making as a norm for noncolonial governments. In its extreme formulation, the concept of neocolonialism betokens utterly dependent government; foreign aid establishes a dependent relationship; therefore the economic development programs of international organizations create neocolonialism.[8]

Such doctrines invoke ideal types. They square poorly with the aims and practices of international organizations. The irreducible doctrinal foundation beneath the policies and practices of these organizations is acknowledgment of a high degree of interdependence among states. The organizations emphasize opportunities for fruitful collaboration, not complete independence of decision-making in national governments. They insist on the need to settle, primarily by compromise, the conflicts that could interfere with cooperation among

[8] For an impassioned, but in my view exaggerated, argument along these lines, see Theresa Hayter, *Aid as Imperialism* (Harmondsworth: Penguin Books, 1971). See also Ronald Nairn, *International Aid to Thailand.*

governments. Although the operational programs of international organizations depend on only a few members for financial support, a symbolic aura of cooperativeness and interdependence, built of small contributions from all members, including recipients of aid, shines over the entire enterprise.

Yet the very governments, including Tanzania and Zambia, that most vociferously insist on independence strictly defined, especially with regard to the governments of Western Europe and the United States, are among the first to demand broader aid programs from international organizations. Paradoxically, obtaining membership in international organizations, despite the implied acceptance of the doctrine of interdependence, figures among the first acts to signify independence on the part of most new states.

In formal terms, it is simple to explain the paradox. The decision-making arrangements of international agencies provide representation in some form for all members and for their views. Thus, new countries mindful of their independence have an opportunity to shape and influence the policies which they will be urged to accept. Formally, they have no need to accept the recommendations. Furthermore, their own contributions to the organizations signify the exercise of independence, not the imposition of restraint from outside sources.

The day-to-day operation of aid programs as well as the requirements of membership in international organizations, as this study will attempt to show, tend to run in a different manner from the formal model. Effective influence in international organizations, especially those dealing with technical subject matters, may require the application of precisely the sort of expertise which is in desperately short supply in most of the LDCs and which their governments seek to acquire through outside aid. Furthermore, decisions in these organizations do not spring phoenix-like from the dregs of faintly parliamentary discussions in the infrequent sessions of general representational organs. Rather, for many practical purposes, decisions emanate from a bureaucracy that is every bit as foreign as that of a far-off country. Finally, the promotion of nationalism by the governments of the LDCs as a means of coping with internal centrifugal forces may also impede easy and enthusiastic cooperation through international organizations.

A second notion central to this study suggests that differences in the doctrinal approaches of the LDCs and the international organizations involve a certain tension. This is simultaneously heightened and kept within bounds by the very pervasiveness and continuing growth of international organization programs and personnel.

Some of this tension results from the difference in approach between organizing the world and organizing the limited area and population of a particular country for the achievement of set goals. Attempts at world organization necessarily must slight some parochial interests, especially when the latter conflict with each other. Such conflicts cannot be avoided in a world with limited resources and vast differences in economic development, not to speak of social values. Furthermore, most of the highly nationalistic governments of new countries aim at development that contrasts sharply with their own immediate past. They seek little less, in some instances, than a social reorganization and the creation of an economic system that is viable in and benefits from an interconnected world of modern economies. Their ultimate goal, however far from achieving it they may be, usually is that of the rich states which provide lavish welfare benefits and which are most proficient in using modern technology, for which interdependent organization is a precondition.

In order to achieve significant progress toward the standards implied by this model, the LDCs almost always seek outside help. For several reasons, some LDCs seek assistance from international organizations in preference to more bountiful bilateral sources. Or they supplement bilateral aid with that from international bodies. The response from the organizations is enthusiastically to proffer whatever their resources will permit.

Successful application for aid from international organizations opens the way for penetration of a government's decision-making process by the organizations. This penetration need not be judged as either pernicious or beneficial of itself: rather, it is a necessary outcome of the expansion of programs by international organizations. Here arise the new problems and tensions regarding the respective roles of international organizations on the one hand, with their limited capacity to command by means of their potential for increasing influence, and of the member-recipients on the other hand, with their jealous view of their own independence and intense needs for outside aid.

On the basis of this reasoning, a third proposition may be stated: the expansion of international organization programs reflects a change (both accomplished and in progress) in the character of their goals and their relations with their members. The credibility of claims about the "nonpolitical" status of the international bodies tends to become diluted. They have in fact become symbolically and practically involved in important political decisions of their members.

Hundreds of resolutions and recommendations concerning economic development and social change have been deliberately drafted in the international institutions that make up the UN system. Some of these are symbols reflecting the ambitions of free-wheeling diplomats. Others represent serious efforts to lay down effective guidelines for the behavior of member governments. Yet others have the effect of orders to the international secretariats. Together they contain the goals and directives that supposedly are to guide the entire UN system.

These doctrinal outpourings raise problems of resource allocation that go to the heart of political life in the LDCs. As early as 1948, the Universal Declaration of Human Rights, adopted without dissent in the UN General Assembly, declared the right of every person to employment, social security, and as much education as he merits. The goals for the First and Second United Nations Development Decades suggested steps by governments to reach specified levels of annual increase in gross national product; for the Second Development Decade, now in progress, it was to be 5 percent annually. Another striking example comes from the Food and Agricultural Organization of the United Nations (FAO), which has elaborated a world development plan for agriculture, the occupation from which the vast majority of the world's people directly derive their sustenance. Goals such as these are supported by the governments of the LDCs, which often manifestly cannot hope to achieve them in the short term, if ever.

19

Where political discussion is permitted, the failure of governments to achieve the goals to which they subscribe could become a domestic issue.

Furthermore, development of field operations suggests that international officials, guided by the doctrines of the UN system, will bring national bureaucracies in touch with controversial new notions. International officials will seek particular stances from their specialized opposite numbers in national bureaucracies. For example, ministries of education maintain close contacts with the UN Education, Scientific, and Cultural Organization (UNESCO). National officials then must react, engage their reputations, and make judgments in close proximity to international officials. In addition, national officials may have direct contacts through attending meetings summoned by international institutions.[9] The resultant interaction can produce a duality of views, on the one side favoring international cooperation and on the other seeking narrow advantage.

The international organizations probably will become ever more deeply involved in the political decisions of their members in the future. Moreover, their operations may increasingly be used in competitions among local political groups. This deepening of political influence should not be viewed as a linear progression. Rather, it proceeds in bursts of activity and intermittent lulls. It differs in varied national contexts. Despite the discontinuity, change in the direction of increasing influence does appear to have taken place in the last two decades and will go on, barring a drastic change in the nature of international politics.

[9] Interesting insights in the interplay of bureaucrats, governments, and international institutions are developed throughout Cox, and Jacobson, *Anatomy of Influence*, especially 380ff.

Discussion of the growth of the activities of international organizations can be related to the functional theory of international organization and its concept of task expansion. In its pristine form, functionalist theory suggests that the world can begin to achieve organization on the basis of whatever cooperation proves possible in any technical field. One act of cooperation paves the way for the next. The need for cooperation and the success of earlier efforts produce task expansion. In the long run, as the habit of international cooperation grows within governments, the resulting interconnectedness binds tighter, until the main decisions of national governments are deeply affected by what international organizations decide and do. Cooperation spills over from one sector to the next, until at last even the intractable decisions affecting peace and security come under the dominant influence of international institutions. This splendidly peaceful outcome derives from strict concentration on the technical jobs at hand. In short, politics can be separated from economics, social change, and technology.

In the UN system, the hypothesis that politics and welfare can be divorced receives only partial acceptance, as the linking of security functions to preconditions of well-being testifies. The cooperative practices intended to promote the general welfare are understood to have a long-term causal relationship to peace, but in addition they can be engaged immediately in the defense of peace in case of aggression.

Other features of the organizational structure argue implicitly for the separability hypothesis. General welfare functions have an organizational locus in the Economic and Social Council that is apart from the security structure. Even if the legal powers given in the Charter are invoked to call for support from the specialized agencies in the case of a breach of the peace, the results are likely to have little short-term effect. But security problems usually pose the need for quick action and quick results. Thus, both structure and reality tend in the direction of treating security problems as different from those of the general welfare.

Recent reconsiderations of functionalist theory raise cutting questions about the separability hypothesis. The basis of this study derives from similar questions. Field research hardly supports the idea that politics and economic and social development differ in kind, either in the world of ideas or in the less tidy world of operating international agencies. The relationship between organizations and governments always has a political nature, whatever the intention may be, for it involves conflict, distribution of values in short supply, imperfect ability to predict outcomes, less than settled doctrines, and the cooperation of institutions created to deal with conflict. But the political relationships involved in international operations to promote the general welfare can be regarded as a distinct variety. It is international and only recent in origin, juxtaposing territorially based and globally based institutions and mixing policies formed at both national and international levels.

Growth and Change of Field Operations

In geographical extent, the field operations of the UN system have reached vast proportions. The UNDP maintains Resident Representatives in some 90 countries and sponsors projects in more than 110. Such projects involve one or several of the specialized agencies of the United Nations itself or the World Bank as executing agencies. The international agencies have furnished nearly 7000 advisers in various categories, who in 1967, for example, served 4500 man-years.

All countries receiving such aid bear the formal classification of "less developed," or "developing," as used in UN documents, although there are wide differences among them. Some, such as Greece and Poland, so closely approach the output and rate of growth of the highly developed countries that it is difficult in the face of the needs of the others to justify aid to them. The LDCs constitute the overwhelming majority of international organization members, a fact which is reflected in the present keen interest of the institutions in problems of development and in assistance to overcome them. Nevertheless, requests for such aid invariably exceed the capacity of the agencies to furnish it.

Even in the short historical perspective of broad-membership international institutions, effectively extending only little more than fifty years, the presence of such numbers of personnel under international auspices and the operation of a program of such a magnitude signify a remarkable change in attitude about what falls within the definition of a domestic problem. Governments continue to guard closely their authority over their territories and peoples, but they have overcome earlier fears about the effects of internationally sponsored activities, or have learned how to adjust to them in order to receive benefits.

Occasionally, but never as a matter of routine, the League of Nations furnished advisers and advisory missions to governments that sought them, usually in time of some emergency, such as the collapse of a banking system or the outbreak of an epidemic. This practice had not been anticipated by the authors of the League of Nations Covenant or the founding members. It grew out of improvised responses to situations of international interest beyond the capacity of a local regime.

The League's sister organization and future participant in the UNDP, the International Labor Organization (ILO), also began in a modest way to furnish advisory services in connection with some social welfare problems. But its main and most familiar procedure remained the creation of international conventions which were intended to regulate the behavior of adhering governments. By this means, the ILO pioneered in opening up new subjects to international regulation and attention. Some of these, such as the nighttime employment of women, lay deep within the jurisdiction of member states; these had to give their assent before the regulations took effect. Although member governments were required to report on what actions they took in considering international regulatory conventions proposed by the ILO, they were not bound to adopt them or to accept outside advisers in giving effect to the rules.

The League of Nations responded in part to its own eclipse by calling attention to its successes in creating international structures for cooperative treatment of problems in social and economic fields. It had indeed been able to organize cooperative efforts to a greater degree than ever before known across a broad front of problems, ranging from control of epidemic disease to revision of prejudicial history textbooks for schools. The framework built up by the League suggested that only the beginnings of the potential for international organization had been uncovered. Its in-house appraisal, carried out by a special committee which reported just before the outbreak of the Second World War, suggested the reorientation of the League to concentrate on the general welfare.[10] It was, however, too late to revive any of the League's former influence.

By the time the United Nations was created in 1945, a short-lived agency, the United Nations Relief and Rehabilitation Administration (UNRRA), had already begun and carried out the largest field operation ever attempted by an international organization.[11] Through its refugee camps in Europe and East Asia flowed millions of persons displaced from their homes during the avalanche of war. The UNRRA chartered ships, stockpiled relief supplies, coped with legal questions, created hospitals, and performed a host of other services, all under international auspices and with a staff of mixed nationalities within the territorial jurisdiction of states. Among its manifold accomplishments was one feature that strongly foreshadowed future international programs. This was its practice of providing technical advisers and some materials to rebuild the industrial machines and commercial networks of the damaged areas.

Despite this immediate experience with field operations, the United Nations Charter, completed in 1945 at San Francisco, looked primarily toward economic cooperation in formally constituted international organs to recommend policies to member governments. Members pledged to try to adhere to the policies but were not obliged to do so. Auxiliary means for executing the

[10] The Bruce Committee Report, *The Development of International Co-operation in Economic and Social Affairs: Report of the Special Committee*, Special Supplement to the Monthly Summary of the League of Nations (Geneva, 1939).

[11] A full account is George Woodbridge et al., *UNRRA: The History of the United Nations Relief and Rehabilitation Administration*, 3 vols. (New York: Columbia University Press, 1950).

policies, such as loans or technical advice, were not specifically excluded. The International Bank for Reconstruction and Development (IBRD) had already been established as a loan agency, but its principal role was seen as reconstruction, and that mainly in highly developed countries. Few envisaged in 1945 that the IBRD would ever be busy in what was then understood as the backward parts of the world. Development there would come, if it did at all, as a concomitant of additional progress in the developed countries, which would invest and otherwise stimulate the less developed.[12]

That the prestige and importance of cooperation for the general welfare were raised to new heights was signified by the establishment of the Economic and Social Council as a principal organ. Its output, moreover, was to be turned into general guidelines through close association with the General Assembly. Some hints of the potential for action on a wide range of problems and for penetrating deep into the previous preserves of the member states could be found in glancing references to economic development and, more explicitly stated, in provisions for the promotion of human rights. The new organization also had the power to create additional specialized agencies, which would serve parallel to it as the ILO had with the League. Furthermore, the United Nations was conceived of as a coordinator for the work of the specialized agencies. It would then serve as the central point for international cooperation for the general welfare and could create a certain efficiency and commonality of action among organizations that otherwise had independent bases, including their own memberships, budgets, and staffs.

[12] Edward S. Mason and Robert E. Asher, *The World Bank Since Bretton Woods* (Washington: Brookings Institution, 1973).

With these structural features and the experience of the prewar generation as foundations, the way opened to the expansion of cooperation for the general welfare. To the existing group of specialized agencies, including those that had survived the war, such as the ILO and the International Telecommunications Union (ITU), and those that had been created or planned during the war, such as the IBRD, UNESCO, and the FAO, the United Nations added others, notably the World Health Organization (WHO).

New, specific policies, generated or reflected in the United Nations structure, promoted additional organizational elaboration. Responding to encouragement from the United States in the form of President Truman's proposal of technical cooperation—Point Four in the list recited in his 1949 inaugural speech—the United Nations pushed ahead with the creation of the Expanded Program of Technical Assistance (EPTA). This program, directed by a Technical Assistance Board on which the United Nations and the cooperating specialized agencies were represented, financed technical assistance services to member governments which requested them. The legal restrictions explicitly set forth at the creation of the EPTA unmistakably demonstrate the caution of the member governments as they faced the expansion of international activities.

Growing interest among some governments of the developed countries and increasing pressure from the LDCs led during the 1950s to the establishment by the IBRD, with encouragement from the United Nations, of the International Finance Corporation (IFC) and the International Development Association (IDA) to supplement the "bankable" loans offered by the main body. Parallel to the Technical Assistance Board, the United

27

Nations Special Fund was established to sponsor "pre-investment" projects lasting over several years and providing surveys, training, and other more elaborate technical aid than the earlier body could. The Special Fund and the Technical Assistance Board were merged in 1966 in the UNDP. All of these organizational arrangements, together with an almost undecipherable collection of other lesser organizations and advisory bodies, constitute a huge network for assisting governments in economic development and social change. Figure A outlines the untidy structure as of 1970.

All told, in 1968 the UNDP spent nearly $200 million per year, and the UN Children's Fund (UNICEF) and the World Food Program (WFP) together spent almost $90 million more on field operations.[13] These sums were drawn from voluntary contributions by governments, over and above their normal budgetary contributions to the specialized agencies to which they belonged. The rate of contribution ranges widely among the donors; the United States contributes as much as 50 percent, but measured in percentage of gross national product, some donors surpass the United States. A large proportion of United Nations members contribute either token amounts or nothing at all. Taking into account the ordinary budgets of the United Nations and the specialized agencies (excluding expenditures for the Relief and Works Agency for Palestine Refugees, which could not be numbered among the development agencies), the network disposed of more than $560 million in 1968 for all economic and social activities. Table A indicates the growth of expenditures over time.

In addition, the lending agencies—the IBRD and its

[13] By 1974 the total budgets for these agencies had surpassed $400 million.

daughters, and the International Monetary Fund (IMF) —furnish some field advisers and supervise the use of loans. By the end of 1970 the lending agencies began expanding their field activities. The strongly supportive attitude of the United States government toward the IBRD in particular and internationally administered aid in general gave this expansion special impetus.

The Field for Observation

The primary observation site employed in this study is that of the capital cities of three Central and East African member governments—Malawi, Tanzania, and Zambia—which have been involved with the UN system of aid for economic development. Much basic data were drawn from close observation of international organization activities in these countries during 1965 and 1966 and again, more briefly, in 1970. At the level of the capital, it was thought, the lines of action and reaction could be clearly discerned and the flow of recommendations, suggestions, and pressures most easily charted as they filtered through governmental and intergovernmental channels. Especially during the earlier period, relatively favorable conditions prevailed for watching the process and progress of relationships between members and the international organizations. The three countries were the locus of visible international activity, particularly with respect to the processes of formulating requests for aid and operating joint international organization-member country programs.

Although each country receiving international aid could be considered a unique entity, nevertheless it was assumed that some common features could be found in all recipient states. A minimum commonality could be

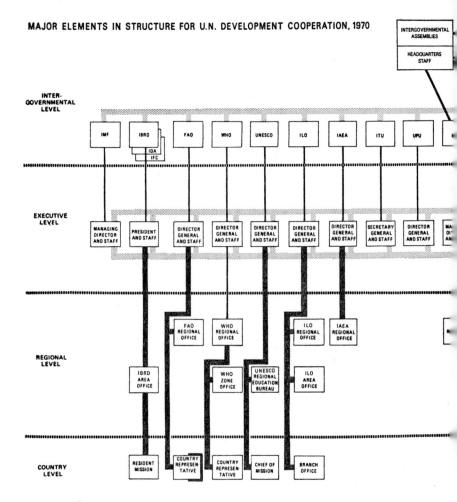

Note:

This chart shows in a skeletal manner the flows of authority and communications among the international agencies of the UN system. Within each level, as well as between levels, communications channels are open but not all are indicated. The chart does not, however, indicate the rate of flow of communications and directives or feedback.

Intergovernmental Level—Each of the agencies represented at this level produces general policy, recommended to governments, and directives for international secretariats. General policies are subjected to efforts at coordination in the Economic and Social Council and the General Assembly. All of the agencies are represented by their chief executive officers on the Administrative Committee for Coordination, which influences the Economic and Social Council and the General Assembly. The flow of communication at this level is highly varied from one agency to the center and among agencies. Generally, however, each

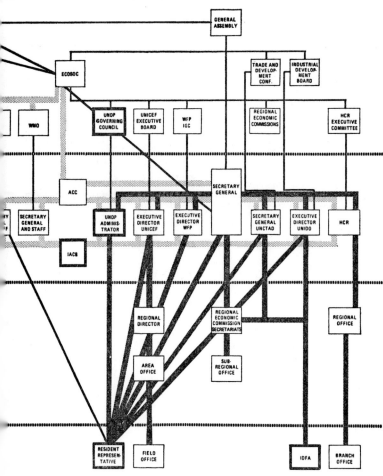

agency tends to emphasize its autonomy whenever it can. Thus, the apparently central position of the General Assembly and the UN Secretary-General reflects a formal arrangement, rather than functional reality.

Executive Level—This includes the executive heads of each agency, variously styled as Secretary-General, Director-General, Managing Director or President, and their international staffs. At this level, the day-to-day direction of operational programs can be found and the direction of communication flows is mainly vertical.

Regional and Country Levels—The field operations with which this study is concerned take place at these levels.

Unfamiliar acronyms—HCR, High Commissioner for Refugees; IACB, Interagency Coordinating Board of UNDP; IAEA, International Atomic Energy Agency; IMCO, Intergovernmental Maritime Consultative Organization; UPU, Universal Postal Union; WMO, World Meteorological Organization.

Source: Chart 7:1, Jackson Report

TABLE A

UN SYSTEM TOTAL NET EXPENDITURE IN ECONOMIC AND SOCIAL ACTIVITIES BY MAIN SOURCES OF FUNDS 1965–1968

(Expressed in $ million)

Agencies or programmes	Total net expenditures				Part financed by UNDP[1]								Breakdown of total net expenditures:							
					Amounts				Percentages of total net expenditures				Financed by regular budget				Financed by extra-budgetary funds			
	1965	1966	1967	1968	1965	1966	1967	1968	1965	1966	1967	1968	1965	1966	1967	1968	1965	1966	1967	1968
UN[2]	84.9	100.0	112.7	128.0	25.6	32.8	37.8	46.0	30	33	34	36	48.9	57.1	63.5	69.2	36.0	42.8	49.2	58.8
FAO	56.4	70.6	77.8	88.5	36.4	47.2	53.5	62.5	65	67	69	71	20.9	24.4	26.2	28.0	35.5	46.2	51.5	60.5
UNESCO	43.7	50.3	54.0	66.5	19.9	25.2	25.8	34.0	46	50	48	51	24.8	26.1	29.6	33.9	18.9	24.2	24.4	32.6
WHO	62.6	74.1	82.7	89.3	8.7	11.4	10.4	13.3	14	15	13	15	38.3	43.4	51.3	55.6	24.2	30.6	31.4	33.8
ILO	31.6	35.6	38.4	44.1	11.7	14.1	15.8	19.1	37	40	41	43	19.2	21.5	23.3	25.6	12.4	14.1	15.1	18.5
IAEA	10.8	12.9	10.6	11.4	1.1	2.0	1.2	2.1	10	15	11	19	7.7	8.7	8.8	9.5	3.2	4.2	1.7	1.9
WMO	3.5	4.7	5.0	7.5	1.8	2.8	2.6	4.5	52	59	52	59	1.3	1.8	2.2	2.7	2.2	2.9	2.8	4.8
ITU	9.5	11.1	11.1	12.3	3.4	4.8	4.8	5.5	36	43	43	44	5.1	5.9	5.7	6.1	4.4	5.2	5.4	6.2
UPU	1.6	2.1	2.2	2.5	0.4	0.6	0.5	0.6	22	27	22	23	1.2	1.4	1.6	1.7	0.4	0.7	0.6	0.8
ICAO	9.1	10.9	9.3	10.8	3.8	4.6	3.7	4.3	42	42	39	40	5.2	6.2	5.6	6.1	3.8	4.7	3.7	4.7
IMCO	0.9	0.9	1.0	1.0	–	0.1	0.1	0.2	3	8	17	20	0.9	0.9	0.8	0.8	–	–	0.2	0.2
Sub-total	314.6	373.1	404.7	462.0	112.9	145.6	156.2	191.7	36	39	39	42	173.6	197.5	218.7	239.3	141.0	175.6	186.0	222.7
UNDP adm.	10.8	13.2	14.7	17.1	10.8	13.2	14.7	17.1	–	–	–	–	–	–	–	–	10.8	13.2	14.7	17.1
UNICEF	30.3	36.2	40.0	45.9	–	–	–	–	–	–	–	–	–	–	–	–	30.3	36.2	40.0	45.9
WFP	18.2	32.0	30.7	50.7	–	–	–	–	–	–	–	–	–	–	–	–	18.2	32.0	30.7	50.7
UNRWA	37.6	37.5	40.5	44.0	–	–	–	–	–	–	–	–	–	–	–	–	37.6	37.5	40.5	44.0
Grand total	411.6	492.0	530.7	619.8	123.7	158.8	170.9	208.8	30	32	32	34	173.6	197.5	218.7	239.3	238.0	294.5	312.0	380.5

[1] UNDP payments to agencies include projects as well as overhead costs; note that UNDP funds are not always presented as extrabudgetary; a number of agencies consider, for instance, the overhead payments as part of their regular budget; this explains why in a few cases the part of TNE financed by UNDP is larger than the total of extrabudgetary funds expended. Also note that UNDP figures do not include payments to IBRD ($2 million in 1965, 3.6 in 1966, 5.1 in 1967 and

[2] Figures include only expenditures attributable to activities in the economic, social and human rights fields. (as per definition adopted by ACC); see source below; totals include UNIDO, UNCTAD, and UNHCR expenditures.
Sources: Expenditures of the UN system in relation to programmes, Annual reports of the ACC (doc. E/4351, E/4501 and E/4702). UNDP statistics.

traced in the existence of separate states claiming legal sovereignty but engaging themselves as members of international organizations. The decision-making and mutual stimulation of activity by member countries and international organizations also could be included among common features. Therefore, the three countries chosen for observation could serve to some extent as microcosms of the recipient government-international organization relationship generally. The extent to which generalizations drawn from this study may stand in the broader universe of all aid recipients cannot be tested here. It remains for study by other researchers undertaking a much more elaborate research program than this one. Yet the generalizations developed here may apply widely for international organization structures and processes that are, it would appear, similar throughout the world. This generality is implicitly accepted in the notion of a program of assistance for economic development and change, administered for all LDCs by international organizations. Without a considerable degree of commonality of structures and processes, no program would be possible.

Many issues of development are also similar. For example, almost all LDCs lack enough trained manpower to carry out their development programs. A resulting issue is whether manpower training deserves priority over, say, creation of an agricultural loan system. All LDCs have large rural populations and some pockets of rapid urbanization. Should the problems of the new cities be emphasized over the advancement of the rural populations? None of them is free of foreign exchange problems, yet choices must be made as to whether attempts to maximize foreign exchange earnings from existing production facilities should have more emphasis than the husbanding of existing reserves for use in entirely new productive lines. Many LDCs face problems of internal integration and development of political institutions. Most of their governments are newly established and are still feeling their way gingerly into contemporary international problems and effective participation in international institutions.

Malawi, Tanzania, and Zambia each have important particularities, but as could be expected, they have certain common features and experiences.[14] All three of them were non-self-governing territories, colonies, protectorates, or trusteeships administered before independence by the United Kingdom. The British colonial service erected in them similar governmental structures and followed like policies concerning such important matters as alienation of lands, financing of development on the basis of local revenue, and creation of local consultative and governmental organs. All three have inherited similar administrative practices and terminology. During the observation period, the habits of the colonial past remained strong in the administrative offices of the independent state successors.

One of the three, Malawi, the smallest in area and the most densely populated, continued to employ

[14] The writings on East and Central Africa are surprisingly extensive. Some useful historical works are: on Tanzania, Zoe Marsh and G. W. Kingsnorth, *An Introduction to the History of East Africa* (Cambridge: Cambridge University Press, 1965), and J. Clagget Taylor, *The Political Development of Tanganyika* (Stanford: Stanford University Press, 1963). On Zambia and Malawi: Thomas M. Franck, *Race and Nationalism: The Struggle for Power in Rhodesia and Nyasaland* (New York: Fordham University Press, 1960); A. J. Hanna, *The Story of the Rhodesias and Nyasaland* (London: Faber, 1960); and Richard Hall, *Zambia* (New York: Praeger, 1965).

British civil servants in the most senior line positions and professional posts of its civil service. It depended on the United Kingdom for an indispensable but gradually diminishing financial support for its operating budget. In the other countries, most expatriates serving in the civil service did so as advisers on fixed-term contracts, not as officers of a recognizable colonial service. Moreover, expatriate officials came from other than the former colonial country. **1929875**

As former parts of the defunct Central African Federation, Malawi and Zambia necessarily had some common experiences in their efforts to gain independence; these are engraved in the memories of some of their leaders. In both, the principal political groups and leadership emerged from a struggle to free their countries of what they understood as domination by Rhodesia and Rhodesians through the machinery of the Federation. The experiences in each country inspired the leaders of the other. Kenneth Kaunda knew of the progress that Dr. Hastings Kamazu Banda was making in Malawi, and the latter had to think about the former's organizing troubles in Zambia. Even after their own and international reactions to the Unilateral Declaration of Independence (UDI) by the Ian Smith government in Salisbury in 1967, Malawi and Zambia remained subject to strong influences from Rhodesia and South Africa because trade routes, suppliers, and communications, links and centers had all tended to locate in the territory of the dominant partner of the former federation.[15]

[15] Zambia bore the brunt of the immediate effects of the international reaction against UDI. For an informed account, which also discusses Tanzanian and Malawian policies, see Richard Hall, *The High Price of Principles: Kaunda and the White South* (London: Hodder & Stoughton, 1969). See also Robert

During the quest for independence in Malawi and Zambia, Tanzania had relatively little to do with its two neighbors. But later, especially after UDI in Rhodesia, Zambia developed close links with Tanzania, based on the latter's support in creating new communications lines to the sea and on some shared ideological concepts. Malawi's relations with Tanzania, however, became exceedingly cold as Prime Minister (and later President) Banda acquired personal power and drove his opponents into exile; some of them received a warm welcome in Tanzania, causing Banda to make extravagant complaints against revolutionary activities of the government in Dar es Salaam.

Banda refused, moreover, to allow Malawi to take economic punishment for the acts of the white Rhodesians, which he claimed to oppose. His government reacted very cautiously to UDI and in fact did drastically rearrange economic relations. Similarly, Malawi did not join Tanzanian and Zambian opposition to South Africa. Rather, Banda became the first head of state in Black Africa to exchange diplomatic representatives with South Africa. The flow of contract laborers from Malawian soil to the mines of the Rand never was interrupted during the period of observation, despite what United Nations resolutions might urge, and the return flow of foreign exchange continued unchecked.

In none of the three countries were there large numbers of white settlers, although some planters and farmers could be found in all three. Zambia, however, had a concentration of largely South African, Rhodesian,

Good, *UDI: The International Politics of the Rhodesian Rebellion* (Princeton: Princeton University Press, 1974).

and English miners in its copper belt. From them came unmistakable evidence of rasping racial prejudice and mean discrimination, which caused frictions of a sort that were not customary in the other two countries. There white men might be supervisors and even plantation owners but not part of teams doing the rough work of mining. Yet the color bar of British colonialism had existed in all three. As a consequence, close friendships and understanding of political aspirations did not commonly develop between former white administrators and rising black elites.

Tanzania (in its earlier form as Tanganyika) has had the longest and closest relationship with international organizations.[16] As a mandated territory of the League of Nations, it was the only one of the three countries which came under the direct scrutiny of an international organization during the interwar period. Because Tanganyika was administered by the United Kingdom as a class B mandate, its future remained indeterminate. The aim of independence hardly entered the picture; rather, suggestions that Tanganyika could be amalgamated with the British colony of Kenya were frequently heard. The League of Nations gave this idea little encouragement. If the League-supervised administration proved less harsh than the earlier German rule, it can hardly be said that Tanganyika prospered as a result.

After the Second World War the United Kingdom placed Tanzania under the United Nations Trusteeship System. Although the new world organization did not divide the Trust Territories into classes which con-

[16] A comprehensive account is B.T.G. Chidzero, *Tanganyika and International Trusteeship* (London: Stevens, 1964).

37

formed roughly to their relative level of development, independence was set as one goal for the future. Meanwhile, British civil servants spoke on behalf of the administration of the Trust Terrritory during meetings of the Trusteeship Council and of the General Assembly. But the advent of the UN system opened the way to more direct contact between the international organization and nonofficial persons in the territory than had ever before been possible. Visiting Missions were dispatched by the Trusteeship Council. They interviewed the present leaders of Tanzania on their home territory and established the links with them that a sympathetic hearing can foster. Such spokesmen as Julius Nyerere, now President of Tanzania, were invited to appear before United Nations organs in New York. This created new precedents for extending the contact of the United Nations with future leaders. The growing closeness of the relationship between the United Nations and Tanganyikan leaders, who were thinking increasingly of independence as a goal to be reached sooner rather than later, speeded the final breaking of colonial ties in 1960, far more quickly than had been expected by the United Nations Visiting Missions and by the British colonial government. Certainly the new state emerged with a government whose knowledge of international organizations extended far beyond that of the leaders of Malawi and Zambia, which became independent states in 1964.

Malawi, Tanzania, and Zambia rank low on any scale of economic development and social modernization (for a complex of reasons that need not be dealt with here). But in Zambia, where the exploitation of copper mines brings a large foreign exchange income, the gross national product per capita was markedly higher than the meager GNP of the other two countries.[17] Despite Zambian mineral production, the vast majority of people there, as in the other two countries, worked as peasant farmers. Nor did the marked superiority of Zambian GNP imply an even distribution of income or the inclusion of much of its territory within a modern economy.

Beginning with the Arusha Declaration in 1967, Tanzania has deliberately emphasized a program described as socialism.[18] This involves nationalization of some industries and state participation in others, thus enabling the government to exert direct influence on the modern sector of the economy. Simultaneously, the government proclaimed a broad program of cooperative production and marketing in an effort to increase the output and value of farming. This program, which implies far-reaching change in the Tanzanian economy while making immediate alterations only in the narrow modern sector, also deemphasizes bilateral foreign assistance, which had not in any case flowed in the quantity that the government had hoped for. According to the Arusha Declaration and President Nyerere, who was responsible for it, Tanzania would now have to depend on local development rather than on imported capital and skills. This outlook is summed up in the slogan, "self-reliance."

[17] GNP per capita in 1967 was estimated as follows: Malawi—$51; Tanzania—$69; Zambia—$298; South Africa—$618.

The value of exports per capita in 1967 was as follows: Malawi—$56; Tanzania—$222; Zambia—$658; South Africa—$1,898.

Figures from *United Nations Statistical Yearbook 1968* (New York: United Nations, 1969).

[18] The Arusha Declaration, reprinted in Julius K. Nyerere, *Freedom and Socialism* (Dar es Salaam: Oxford University Press, 1968), 231–50, had intellectual roots in other expression by Nyerere. See Bienen, *Tanzania*, 211–26.

Without so explicit an ideological framework, Zambia, too, has rapidly moved toward state participation in modern enterprises, especially in the copper mining industry. It has created a network of state corporations, in which the voice of the government can be heard, both for participation in industry and for sponsorship of new development. Even if Zambian leaders do not make the same point of "self-reliance" as does President Nyerere, they clearly had no intention of permitting unguided expansion of the modern sector or unplanned investment from abroad; rather, they sought to create more economic development from locally derived sources in which the government participates. Without giving sharp definition, or perhaps without even meaning the same thing, both governments spoke of African socialism as a goal.

Such terms did not characterize the approach to development in Malawi. Development plans were less explicit and given less emphasis there. Although a state development corporation provided some state participation, the government did not seek wide powers over what little industry and trade there was. Rather a more nearly laissez-faire approach prevailed, and investments, even from the South African sources that are anathema in Tanzania and Zambia, were welcomed.

Tanzania has become one of the most important African consumers of internationally sponsored technical assistance and preinvestment programs. With a larger population than either Zambia or Malawi and a government that sought for several years to make up dropping foreign exchange earnings, Tanzania at first outstripped the other two countries in the size of its international agency programs. Malawi earned the least foreign exchange of the three and has had far less aid from international agencies. Table B indicates the relative sizes of recent programs supported by the UNDP, the main purveyor of technical assistance and preinvestment projects.

Both Tanzania and Zambia received assistance from international organizations for multicountry or regional projects of considerable size. Such projects had encouragement in the official recommendations of the UNDP, and seven investment projects were supported by the UNDP or other multilateral bodies in the East African region, which includes Tanzania. Zambia inherited participation in two UNDP projects from the Central African Federation, but as a reaction to the Rhodesian UDI, both of them were moved entirely to Zambia, where they were still active in 1970.

Only one of the three countries, Zambia, benefited from a "bankable" loan from the IBRD. As with the Central African regional preinvestment projects, this loan, made for the construction of the Kariba Dam on

TABLE B

Part I

PROJECT EXPENDITURES BY UNDP
1959–1973
(in thousands of dollars)

	Annual Averages		
	1959–63	1964–68	1969–73
Malawi	—	399	1,099
Tanzania	371	1,533	2,465
Zambia	52	542	2,642
All Africa	7,019	30,360	62,920

Source: UN Doc. DP/48/Annex 1, 5 April 1974, p. 8.

41

TABLE B
Part II

PREINVESTMENT PROJECTS SUPPORTED BY UNDP
as of 30 June 1969

Project	Agency	Approved by Governing Council	Project duration (years)	PROJECT COSTS (US dollar equivalent)		
				Total	Governing Council earmarkings	Government counterpart contribution
MALAWI						
Land and Water Resources Development in Southern Malawi	FAO	Jan. 1966	4	3,826,500	2,623,500	1,203,000
Improvement of Livestock and Dairy Production	FAO	June 1968	3	470,100	317,100	153,000
Labor Statistics Unit	ILO	June 1968	3	391,800	248,800	143,000
Fishermen's Training Project	FAO	Jan. 1969	2	525,200	375,200	150,000
TANZANIA, UNITED REPUBLIC OF						
Survey and Plan for Irrigation Development in the Pangani and Wami River Basins	FAO	Jan. 1964	3	2,146,300	1,225,300	921,000
				1,010,500	625,500	385,000

Management, Mweka

Kitulo Sheep-Raising Project	FAO	Jan. 1965	5	1,951,400	964,400	987,000
Training of Secondary School Science Teachers at the Faculty of Science of the University College, Dar es Salaam	UNESCO	Jan. 1965	5½	3,978,600	978,600	3,000,000
Industrial Studies and Development Center, Dar es Salaam	UNIDO	Jan. 1965	5	1,290,000	1,000,000	290,000
National Institute for Productivity, Dar es Salaam	ILO	Jan. 1965	5	1,185,500	860,500	325,000
Work-Oriented Adult Literacy Pilot Project	UNESCO	June 1966	5	6,397,900	1,181,900	5,216,000
Forest Industries Development Planning	FAO	Jan. 1967	3	1,269,900	769,900	500,000
National Industrial Apprenticeship Scheme	ILO	June 1967	5	1,030,100	820,100	210,000
Livestock Development in Masailand, Gogoland and Sukumaland	FAO	June 1968	5	2,464,800	1,409,800	1,055,000
Improvement of Tick Control Methods, Mwanza	FAO	Jan. 1969	4	872,100	531,100	341,000
ZAMBIA						
Multipurpose Survey of the Kafue River Basin	FAO	May 1961	4	1,375,100	786,100	589,000

TABLE B, *Part II* (*cont.*)

PREINVESTMENT PROJECTS SUPPORTED BY UNDP

as of 30 June 1969

Project	Agency	Approved by Governing Council	Project duration (years)	PROJECT COSTS (US dollar equivalent)		Government counterpart contribution
				Total	Governing Council earmarkings	
Training of Secondary School Teachers at the University of Zambia, Lusaka	UNESCO	June 1966	5	6,356,600	1,156,600	5,200,000
Forest Industries Feasibility Study	FAO	Jan. 1967	3½	1,756,800	805,800	951,000
Small-Scale Irrigation Development and Training	FAO	Jan. 1967	3	1,625,600	625,600	1,000,000
National Industrial Vocational Training Scheme	ILO	Jan. 1968	5	3,424,300	1,256,300	2,168,000
Detailed Mineral Exploration West of Broken Hill	UN	Jan. 1968	3½	1,485,000	739,000	746,000
Luangwa Valley Conservation and Development	FAO	Jan. 1968	3½	3,735,400	1,056,400	2,679,000
Central Fisheries Research Institute, Chilanga	FAO	June 1968	4	2,305,400	1,054,400	1,251,000
National Food and Nutri-	FAO	Jan. 1969	3	1,217,500	646,500	571,000

Industries

Regional

Hydrometeorological Survey of the Catchments of Lakes Victoria, Kioga, and Albert[1]	WMO	Jan. 1966	5	4,173,900	1,937,900	2,236,000
East African School of Aviation, Nairobi[2]	ICAO	June 1966	6	2,847,500	984,500	1,863,000
African Development Bank: Preinvestment Unit[3]	UN	Jan. 1967	5	4,901,000	2,993,000	1,908,000
Immunological Research on Tick-Borne Cattle Diseases and Tick Control[3]	FAO	Jan. 1967	3	847,800	554,800	293,000
Transport Study[3]	IBRD	Jan. 1967	1½	875,000	675,000	200,000
Lake Kariba Fisheries Research Institute[4]	FAO	Jan. 1962	4	1,107,200	555,200	552,000
Secondary School Teacher Training[4,5]	UNESCO	June 1963	5	3,373,300	991,300	2,382,000
East African Livestock Plan[6]	FAO	June 1964	1	358,900	238,900[5]	120,000
Lake Victoria Fisheries Research[6]	FAO	Jan. 1965	5	1,359,000	779,000	580,000
East African Railways and Harbors Training and Development[6]	UN	June 1968	5	2,834,000	1,409,000	1,425,000

Project	Agency	Approved by Governing Council	Project duration (years)	PROJECT COSTS (US dollar equivalent)		
				Total	Governing Council earmarkings	Government counterpart contribution
Survey of Transport Studies in Africa[7]	IBRD	June 1968	1	407,000	357,000	50,000
Tanzania-Zambia Railway Link[8]	ADB	June 1968	1	407,800	297,800	110,000
Research on African Migratory Locusts[9]	FAO	Jan. 1969	3	1,181,500	656,500	525,000

[1] Participants: Kenya, Sudan, Uganda, UAR, and Tanzania.

[2] Participants: Kenya, Uganda, and Tanzania.

[3] Tanzania among 14 participants.

[4] Participants: Zambia and United Kingdom on behalf of Rhodesia.

[5] Relocated at Lusaka.

[6] Participants: Kenya, Uganda, and Tanzania.

[7] Covers all countries and territories in Africa, excluding South Africa, Rhodesia, and the Portuguese territories.

[8] Participants: Tanzania and Zambia.

[9] Participants: Cameroon, Central African Republic, Chad, Congo (Brazzaville), Congo (Dem. Rep. of), Dahomey, Gambia, Ghana, Kenya, Ivory Coast, Mali, Mauritania, Niger, Nigeria, Sierra Leone, Senegal, Sudan, Tanzania, Uganda, and Upper Volta.

Source: UN Doc. DP/SF/Reports, Series B, No. 8, as of 30 June 1969.

Table B, *Part III*

COMPARISON OF EXPENDITURES ON UNDP PROJECTS 1961-67

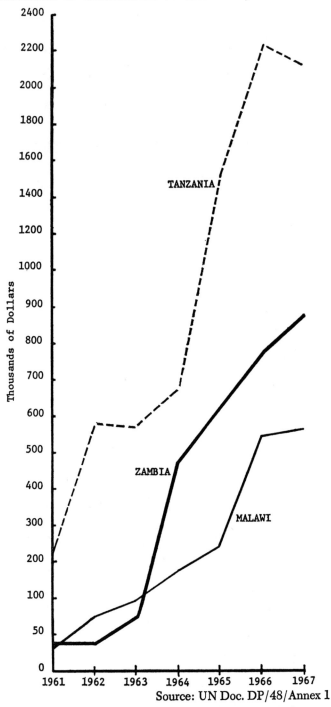

Source: UN Doc. DP/48/Annex 1

TABLE C

WORLD BANK LOANS AND IDA CREDITS BY COUNTRY AS OF 31 DECEMBER 1970
(Expressed in US Dollars)

	Bank Loans		IDA Credits		Total	
	Number	Net Amount[1]	Number	Net Amount[1]	Number	Net Amount[1]
MALAWI	–	–	6	32,750,000	6	32,750,000
TANZANIA[3]	3	42,200,000	9	57,400,000	12	99,600,000
ZAMBIA[4]	11	168,250,000	–	–	11	168,250,000
	14	$ 210,450,000	13	$ 90,150,000	27	$ 300,600,000
AFRICA						
Algeria	3	80,500,000	–	–	3	80,500,000
Botswana	–	–	2	6,100,000	2	6,100,000
Burundi	1	4,800,000	3	3,280,000	4	8,080,000
Cameroon	5	37,100,000	4	28,500,000	9	65,600,000
Central African Rep.	–	–	2	8,500,000	2	8,500,000
Chad	–	–	2	5,900,000	2	5,900,000
Congo, Dem. Rep. of	5	91,582,854	2	11,000,000	7	102,582,854
Cong, People's Rep. of	1	30,000,000	2	2,130,000	3	32,130,000
Dahomey	–	–	2	8,100,000	2	8,100,000
Ethiopia	11	97,800,000	5	35,000,000	16	132,800,000

Gabon	4	54,788,722	–	–	4	54,788,722
Gambia, The	–	–	1	2,100,000	1	2,100,000
Ghana	2	53,000,000	5	24,800,000	7	77,800,000
Guinea	2	64,500,000	–	–	2	64,500,000
Ivory Coast[2]	7	48,491,567	–	–	7	48,491,567
Kenya[3]	11	205,824,026	11	61,300,000	22	267,124,026
Lesotho	–	–	1	4,100,000	–	–
Liberia	4	15,249,802	–	–	4	15,249,802
Malagasy Republic	3	11,100,000	4	29,100,000	7	40,200,000
Mali[2]	–	–	2	16,800,000	2	16,800,000
Mauritania	1	66,000,000	2	9,700,000	3	75,700,000
Mauritius	1	6,973,119	–	–	1	6,973,119
Morocco	9	151,720,830	2	18,300,000	11	170,020,830
Niger	–	–	3	8,203,224	3	8,203,224
Nigeria	11	251,600,000	2	35,500,000	13	287,100,000
Rhodesia[4]	3	86,950,000	–	–	3	86,950,000
Rwanda	–	–	1	9,300,000	1	9,300,000
Senegal[2]	2	7,500,000	3	17,100,000	5	24,600,000
Sierra Leone	3	11,400,000	2	6,500,000	5	17,900,000
Somalia	–	–	3	9,050,000	3	9,050,000
South Africa	11	241,800,000	–	–	11	241,800,000
Sudan	6	129,000,000	2	21,500,000	8	150,500,000
Swaziland	2	6,950,000	1	2,800,000	3	9,750,000
Togo	–	–	1	3,700,000	1	3,700,000

Table C

World Bank Loans and IDA Credits by Country as of 31 December 1970
(Expressed in US Dollars)

	Bank Loans		IDA Credits		Total	
	Number	Net Amount[1]	Number	Net Amount[1]	Number	Net Amount[1]
Tunisia	9	70,935,480	5	39,962,598	14	110,898,078
Uganda[3]	1	8,400,000	6	37,000,000	7	45,400,000
United Arab Rep.	1	56,500,000	1	26,000,000	2	82,500,000
Upper Volta[2]	–	–	2	7,000,000	2	7,000,000
Bank Total, 88 Countries + IFC	725	$14,646,682,507				
IDA Total 55 Countries			237	$2,886,129,956		
Combined Bank/IDA Total 104 Countries + IFC						
TOTAL (Bank and IDA)					962	$17,532,812,463

[1] Net of cancellations, refundings, and terminations.

[2] One loan for $7.5 million shown against Ivory Coast is shared with Mali, Senegal and Upper Volta.

[3] Six loans aggregating $162.8 million shown against Kenya are shared with Tanzania and Uganda.

[4] Three loans totaling $106.7 million have been assigned in equal shares to Rhodesia and Zambia.

Source: Policies and Operations; The World Bank, IDA and IFC (Washington: International Bank for Reconstruction and Development, 1971).

the Zambezi River—vital still as the main supplier for electric power for the operation of the Zambian copper industry—also involved Rhodesia. All three countries, however, have received "soft" loans from the IBRD subsidiary, the IDA. Recent statements by IBRD President Robert McNamara indicate that this category of aid may increase. But the three countries certainly could not be characterized as leading borrowers from the international lending agencies. (See table C.)

Thus, despite many differences, the three countries had strong common elements and outlooks in relation to the economic development programs of international organizations. They clearly appeared as the most welcome kind of applicant, given their developmental status and their new statehood, for technical assistance under international organization programs; and this could lead to capital assistance from the financial agencies. National development programs would create relationships with the international organizations and also produce, perhaps, some visible patterns of mutual influence.

2.

STRUCTURAL COUNTERPARTS

T HE process of securing assistance from an international organization involves a national governmental hierarchy and the counterpart hierarchies of one or several international organizations. These hierarchies reflect the modes of operation thought appropriate by the founders of the international organizations and by the national governments. The original approaches were set forth in formal, legal documents that emerged from the policy-making negotiations of the international organizations. But elaborations of these approaches emerged in practice and became the basis, and to a considerable extent the boundary markers, of the field programs. This chapter therefore begins with a consideration of the formally designed structures and describes how the national and international hierarchies operating within them have created parallel ladders of access to one another's processes.[1]

The formal, legal relationships of member governments and international organizations—set forth in con-

---

[1] This study deals mainly with what Cox and Jacobson, *Anatomy of Influence*, 5, have called the service functions of international organizations. They point out that not all signatories of constitutional documents for international organizations have similar conceptions of the agreements and that not all their ambitions are contained in such documents. It is fair to say that most of the work dealt with here falls into the unanticipated category with regard to the organizations which antedated the growth of technical assistance after 1950.

stitutional documents and other rules—fit squarely into diplomatic and international legal experience. As sovereigns, the member governments agree to limit their range of actions in particular ways in order to create international institutions and to operate them. Membership is voluntary and so for the most part is cooperation within a given organization. Each member is represented in the final organ of decision, usually that which gives the last formal approval to the budget of the organization. Members may also be represented on subsidiary and specialized organs of various kinds, if they wish to serve. Finances derive from contributions by members; these contributions are required by membership but can exceed minimum quotas on a voluntary basis. Member governments alone consent to the presence of international organization personnel and programs on their territory. Each government must specifically request such activity and agree to permit it to go on. Although international organizations offer a variety of services, no government is obliged to seek or accept any or all of them, nor can any international organization legally impose its service on members, even if it had sufficient force to do so. Some governments, such as that of Burma, have suspended the activities of international agencies because of domestic factors. Others have cut short particular activities, as Guinea did when it abruptly sent away a Personal Representative of the UN Secretary-General.

For their part, international organizations do not formally support governments. They sometimes support programs set up by national governments, but this aid is defined in terms of specific projects which are carefully limited in scope and duration. International agencies formally reject requests that are not made in the

53

proper form on behalf of the government concerned. If initiation and formulation of a request for assistance belong within the responsibility of a member government, it follows that the international organizations have, formally speaking, only a reactive role in the relationship; they remain passive until a government makes a request.

Once the formal process of granting aid has been initiated by a member government, then the international organizations must make decisions and distinctions that cannot help but influence the plans of the government. In its simplest form, this influence derives from the decision to grant the requested assistance or to refuse it. A negative decision clearly would force the government seeking aid to revise its plans.

Negative decisions necessarily emerge from the international organizations, no matter how much the membership may want expansion of aid programs. Resources are too limited to honor all requests, and they are likely to remain limited, so that the selectivity of the decision process must continue in some form. Furthermore, the final decision to honor a request for aid or to deny it, whether formally registered in the Governing Council of the UNDP or by the Executive Directors of the IBRD, involves preliminary analysis and recommendation from a secretariat. The secretariat usually takes pride in its independence and expert knowledge. For ostensibly technical reasons, some requests will not be honored at all, on the advice of the secretariat. Others will be brought before the formal decision-making body by the secretariat only if they are altered in specified ways.

The formal, legal arrangements in fact opened the way for offering rewards for approved kinds of development policies and for withholding rewards from governments which fail to adopt those policies. Such rewards and penalties bear no explicit designation and do not necessarily even find a place in the formal structures. Rather, the official position states that technical and economic considerations provide the only bases for the allocation of resources.

Dealing with international organizations is for recipient governments a matter much closer to home than a headquarters establishment in some distant capital. On the territories of the recipient governments, international agencies usually make use of some sort of representation, apart from international civil servants furnishing direct economic development services. The most notable variety of these representatives is the UNDP Resident Representative, who has the formal right to be treated as the senior official among those present from international agencies, some of which go to considerable lengths to emphasize their autonomy.

Under UNDP rules, to which a recipient government must agree, the government formally designates a channel through which all business with the international organization is conducted. This could be the Ministry of Foreign Affairs, a technical ministry, or a planning agency, depending upon the particular circumstances and the nature of the work involved. As compared with the usual method of handling foreign relations through the foreign affairs ministry exclusively, there is a certain flexibility here which, nevertheless, ends in a formal relationship. At the same time, all international organization representatives operate at the pleasure of the host government and must have a traditional diplomatic *agrément* from the government before taking up their duties.

International organization officials in the economic development field have no general mandate to seek "diplomatic" and representational duties. Nevertheless, their work is sheltered by certain privileges and immunities common to diplomatic intercourse. From the point of view of an international agency, these special provisions equalize working conditions from one country to another and establish a certain parity with employees of bilateral programs. What is symbolically more important, officials are protected from arbitrary interference by the host government. From the point of view of the government, such privileges serve to mark out international officials as a specific group to which a separate legal regime applies and which can therefore be treated differently from national officials doing similar work. Whatever the practical effect of such privileges and immunities, it is always clear that they relate to the work of officials, not to their persons as representatives of a sovereign.

Relations with and assistance provided by international agencies are subjects of a formal agreement between them and each recipient state. Sometimes this agreement takes a general, standard form and sometimes it is made *ad hoc* for a specific project with exceptional features. All such agreements spell out the nature of the relationship and of the assistance which will be offered, the conditions under which it is to be furnished, the duties of the recipient government with regard to receiving and using the aid, the duration of the agreement, and the conditions under which it may be discontinued or changed. It can be likened in form and content to a treaty. When a standard form is used, the recipient government must satisfy itself that it could gain no advantages from negotiating a special document. Where an *ad hoc* agreement is made, each side seeks to satisfy its own policy needs, while leaving some possibility for acceptance by the other party. The international agencies aim primarily at suitable conditions for their operations, which usually means as little as possible in the way of day-to-day or unilateral alteration of the projects by the recipient government.

In many important respects, the outward form of a relationship between an intergovernmental aid agency and a recipient government resembles the conventional arrangements made between sovereign governments for cooperative ventures. But, in fact, both the subject and the institutional forms of the agency-government arrangement differ from the conventional model. The subject matter involves the allocation of financial resources, as it might in a bilateral aid agreement. But in the case of an international agency, the recipient government usually is a member of the international organization. Thus, it has a responsibility of some sort for the organization to which it applies for aid. In some cases, the representatives of an applicant government serve on the Governing Council of the UNDP or similar supervisory bodies in other agencies.

Thus, the prospective recipient seeks aid to which it has a rightful claim as an organization member, provided it meets certain conditions which it may itself have helped design and approve. This obviously differs from the more loosely organized negotiations that take place between governments. Furthermore, in the international realm, decisions on allocation of resources formally emerge from collegial consideration by several governments. More than two-party agreement is required in all but minor cases (when the secretariat has power, subject to review, to make decisions). The style of decision-making fits less well with a model of diplomatic bargaining than it does with a model of a series of deliberative organs.

STRUCTURES FOR AID REQUESTS

Specific requests for aid from international organizations develop through structures which lie mainly within the administrative establishments of national governments. International organizations do not create machinery parallel to all of that of national governments and certainly do not have such large numbers of personnel at their disposal. The national and international structures meet formally and, to a considerable degree, in fact, in the office of the Resident Representative or other local representative of an international body, e.g., the regional office of the IBRD or the country representative of the WHO.

The formal progress of an aid request followed the same general pattern in each of the three countries studied and was probably similar to that of most aid recipients. Initiatives to seek international aid develop within the normal government machinery, either as part of planning or as an offshoot of operations which, it is believed, could be improved with outside resources. The rationale for such aid in all cases is the claim that the national government cannot otherwise procure the financing or service that is essential to a development plan. The aid usually is intended to contribute to a project which can be partly supported by local resources. Only after the request takes a form which satisfies the substantive ministries concerned does it come into the purview of the special national machinery created within the administration for dealing with international agencies.

This machinery often can be found in or closely related to the ministry or office which concerns itself with the national plan. It is charged with coordinating, not originating, requests for technical assistance. Everyone concerned with the process, however, understands that coordination necessarily involves determining priorities. The officials in the coordination body are expected to know what sorts of projects fall within the interests of which specific international organizations and to separate the projects appropriate for bilateral programs from those which would prove most attractive to multilateral agencies. Loans, however, are almost always handled separately by the finance ministry. Requests for aid or loans are generally forwarded only after a decision by the cabinet grants them official government sanction and political support.

Despite the ease with which the general pattern can be discerned, specific differences among the governments of Malawi, Tanzania, and Zambia and their specific policies had special importance for the initiation of international aid projects. These differences, disclosed by observation in the field, concern the nature of specific machinery, its place within the government hierarchy, the state of national planning, the character of the national plan, and the domestic political configurations during the observation period.

Ministries headed by members of the cabinet had charge of planning in Tanzania and Malawi, although national planning in Tanzania previously had been a responsibility of the presidential office. The creation of a planning ministry in Malawi was so recent that the pattern of its development was unclear. In Zambia, the Office of National Development and Planning was an adjunct of the presidency and headed by a recently appointed Zambian permanent secretary. In all three cases, then, national planning had enough importance to be formally represented at the top of the government. The perception by the governments that a planning effort helps to attract foreign aid may be counted as one of the reasons for its apparent importance in the formal structure.

In Tanzania and Zambia, planning was intended to include control of ministerial expenditures on the basis of specified projects outlined in comprehensive, published plans.[2] Both plans contained sectoral targets and looked ahead to structural changes in the economy and society. These changes were intended both to modernize productive relationships within the economy and to increase the overall output. The general relationships between sectors of the economy and the goals within them were set out with some specificity. Because both governments sought as a high priority goal to achieve a higher level of economic development and because both regarded planning as an important means to this end, their national plans reflected and incorporated some of their most important political goals.

Since then, both Tanzania and Zambia have shifted away from these plans, which bore the heavy imprint of economists trained in the western European and

[2] *Five-Year Plan for Economic and Social Development*, 2 vols. (Dar es Salaam: Government Printer, 1964); and Office of National Planning and Development, *First National Development Plan 1966–1970* (Lusaka: Government Printer, 1966). See Bienen, *Tanzania*, chapter VIII, for an excellent account of the formulation of the Tanzanian plan.

North American modes of analysis and theory. With the Arusha Declaration, the Nyerere government in Tanzania downgraded earlier plans for rapid industrialization or modernization aided by heavy foreign investment. Instead, it chose to emphasize improvement of peasant farming, creation of cooperative structures, and financial self-reliance. The idea of national planning survived, and international agencies have reacted with equanimity to the new Tanzanian approach. Similarly, in Zambia, the government chose to emphasize participation in ownership in foreign concerns, including the copper mines, and has developed an elaborate mechanism for the purpose. Such a move does not necessarily negate the goals established in earlier plans, but it implies quite different methods of financing development. In both instances, it is fair to say, the earlier plans have been sharply downgraded as guides to governmental policy.

The Malawi plan contrasted sharply with those of Tanzania and Zambia in both form and content.[3] It was a fifteen-page, summary document, providing little elaboration of the goals set by the government of President H. Kamazu Banda, which had produced no coherent statement of development aims, aside from its refusal to break off economic ties with South Africa and Rhodesia. The plan projected social and economic change only in the most general way, largely by implication, and its economic analysis and statistical content were minimal (although, given the unreliability and spottiness of statistics generally in Africa, this may have little real effect). Most of the document consisted of a list of projects which the government hoped to carry out,

[3] *Development Plan* 1965–1969 (Zomba: Government Printer, 1964).

61

if aid were made available. In all, the plan resembled a shopping list, developed by civil servants in ministries, with few marks of the professional planner and fewer still of coherent government plans for economic development. It was expected, however, that closer attention to planning would result from the establishment of a Ministry of Development and Planning and the introduction of more skilled economic analysts. At the same time, an observer could not overlook the paramount position of the president in all matters of government expenditure and his willingness to put aside reasoned bureaucratic papers in order to conduct personal policies.

Precisely where the planning function is located in government structure has an important bearing on whether it will be treated as the obscure duty of specialized bureaucrats or as an important means of guiding policy. In Zambia and Malawi, national planning reports were signed by government ministers. Consideration of these reports brought cabinet-level attention to bear on revisions of the plan and problems of execution, including the resulting relationship with international organizations. National planning in Tanzania either was managed as part of the president's office, under close direction of a minister, or was given to an independent ministry headed by a person closely identified with the president. In Zambia and Tanzania, a system of regional development committees, made up of key local personnel, including dignitaries of the governing political party, was supposed to extend knowledge of and garner support for the national plan. Thus, a political base for development in accordance with a national plan was projected.[4] At the same time, it was

[4] Bienen, *Tanzania*, trenchantly demonstrates the thinness of

obvious that only a limited number of ministers and civil servants, aside from even less sophisticated party rank-and-filers, had a working grasp of economic planning. Moreover, the political sensitivity of economic development tended to push decisions upward in the hierarchy, where the influential or dominant views of the president often became involved.

From the point of view of international organizations offering aid, these nascent planning mechanisms were beginning to produce information relevant to their mode of work. Even the most rudimentary planning has the effect of identifying specific development projects. Such identification is a necessary first step toward the initiation and preparation of requests to international agencies. Only specific, well-defined projects received support. Therefore, planning staffs tended to become involved, often crucially, in projects sponsored by international organizations.

This involvement had a formal basis in Zambia and Malawi, where the planning offices were charged with coordinating foreign aid, except loans, which were dealt with in the finance ministries. One result of vesting the coordinating function in the planning office was that the civil servants and foreign advisers who specialized in national planning, who had responsibility for coordinating the development projects generated in ministries, and who had overall supervisory duties on specific projects also tended to become the central and most expert sources of information and techniques for dealing with international organizations. Along with the formal responsibility of framing requests for aid, they

---

this process in Tanzania. It was certainly even less developed in Zambia (and nonexistent in Malawi).

maintained liaison with local representatives of international agencies when the requests were made.

In Tanzania, the structure was somewhat different. Responsibility for coordination was assigned to the Ministry of Finance, which had long been powerful in the government. Although it was difficult to estimate how effectively the treasury and the economic ministry were linked, centralization in the finance ministry of duties involving international aid resulted in a close connection between efforts to secure financing from international sources and to obtain other sorts of aid, such as preinvestment surveys. Because such projects can lead to requests for loans, there was an obvious rationale for this pattern of organization.

In some instances, the foreign ministries had duties that related to requests for aid, and they advised on the sources to which applications were made. As one high official in Tanzania remarked: "Aid may have ties, but receiving it also may give us some political influence. We look to see if we can get any significant influence by taking aid from one donor rather than another." Other ministries whose programs would benefit from a successful application may also comment formally or informally during the process of developing a request. A high value was placed on coordination; requests went forward with as broad a measure of agreement as possible in the governments and civil services.

However, a mere description of the form of the government structures dealing with planning and with international aid must mislead unless the actual situation within the ministries is taken into account. If the established structures functioned efficiently and precisely on the basis of good information, the result would conform to the textbook model. In fact, the operations were hardly model, for reasons that begin with insufficiencies and inexperience. All three countries lacked adequate statistics and other kinds of knowledge about themselves. They suffered equally from debilitating shortages of skilled manpower. Many high-level posts in the civil service, and especially in the relatively new ministries employing concepts unfamiliar during the colonial period, went unmanned or were occupied by very young men with little training and even less experience. Officials trained in economics and statistics or with high level administrative experience relevant to international organization affairs were in especially short supply (although the concentration on education and training during the last decade is gradually producing more qualified officials). Many important offices still were headed by expatriates. Some of these officials came on the scene as advisers on narrow technical problems, but they nevertheless soon had close connections with operations.

The very process of planning for development and working with international organizations represented innovation in these countries; its techniques often appeared arcane to officials and political leaders newly introduced to them. Political leaders, furthermore, not infrequently regarded planning (and the research that must go with it) as over-sophisticated, excessively intellectualized exercises that do not produce "action" in the form of tangible benefits.

ACCESS FOR INTERNATIONAL ORGANIZATION PERSONNEL

Through national planning structures and the formal drafting of aid requests a number of relationships develop between the national civil services and political leaders and the international organization representatives. These relationships provide a means of access for international organizations to national decision-making processes and serve as one stimulus to the growth of informal associations. For international organization personnel, access is in fact manifold and multidirectional; it occurs at a large number of points and at different levels in the national hierarchy. In general, it has not been disturbed by unfavorable attitudes and protective administrative measures; it has a background of more than two decades and a thick overlay of policies. Such continuing programs and precedents tend to open additional opportunities to expand access.

Even before the independence of Tanzania and Zambia, the foundation for access by international organizations was established. In the former, the IBRD carried out and published a major economic survery.[5] By providing intellectual impetus that on the whole was lacking during most of the colonial period and by building up new knowledge (or published guesses, in some cases), this report moved the government toward early adherence to the idea of development planning and signaled the possible growing importance of aid from international organizations. In Zambia, the United Nations, together with the FAO, produced the first economic survey of real breadth and depth.[6] It served the new government, which subsequently brought the country to independence, with an initial formulation of

[5] IBRD Economic Survey Mission to Tanganyika, *The Economic Development of Tanganyika* (Baltimore: Johns Hopkins University Press, 1961).

[6] United Nations, UN Economic Commission for Africa, Food and Agriculture Organization of the UN, *Economic Development of Zambia* (Ndola: Falcon Press, 1964).

66

development priorities and projects and offered the basis for a transitional national plan.

As a result of these reports, two of the three countries came to independence with some civil servants, for the most part expatriates, who were accustomed to close association with international agencies in development planning. In addition, the international organizations subsequently were favored by generally receptive government policies. In all three countries, but especially in Tanzania and Zambia during the period of observation, political leaders and civil servants at all levels hewed to the doctrine that international organizations offer assistance that is both free of political implications and an alternative to bilateral aid. The latter drew particular suspicion for its alleged leverage on policies outside the development field, especially with regard to issues that involved the Cold War. As a foreign office official in Dar es Salaam remarked, aid from international organizations fits with a nonaligned political stance and is therefore preferable, even if more substantial projects can sometimes find backing from bilateral sources.

The UN system acted to take advantage of the favorable postindependence attitude with which it was viewed in the three countries by creating special representational arrangements. In Tanganyika, the first to gain independence, a conventional Resident Representative's office was placed in operation to serve the UN Technical Assistance Board (UNTAB) and the UN Special Fund. In 1962, it was taken over by George Ivan Smith, a high-ranking UN official who had worked closely with Secretary-General Dag Hammarskjöld in the Middle East in 1956. His experience was mainly in public relations and political affairs, some of it in the

Congo, where he had acquired a deep interest in the new politics of postcolonial Africa. As head of the office in Dar es Salaam, he was styled Personal Representative of the Secretary-General, an unusual title signifying a direct relationship with the Secretary-General and a broad mandate. Other officials granted such a title for assignments in the aid field were given primarily political tasks.[7] Ivan Smith headed UNTAB and Special Fund activities not only in Tanganyika, but also in the other two countries of East Africa, Kenya and Uganda, which had not then achieved formal independence. Negotiations between the United Nations and the three governments before the establishment of his office led to an understanding that as Personal Representative Ivan Smith would have access to the heads and ministers of government, as if he were a national ambassador. At the same time, he would have the normal responsibilities of a Resident Representative.

In Tanganyika, Ivan Smith did in fact establish close relationships with President Nyerere and the ministers who had important roles in the development field. He discussed more general political matters with the president and his advisers and sent frequent reports to the Secretary-General. He saw his role as that of a political observer in East Africa, where he could watch the unfolding of decolonization and development of regional politics. The backwash of events in the Congo troubled the entire area, and the governments defined and redefined attitudes toward their giant neighbor as its troubles multiplied. Refugees spilled over the borders,

[7] For further discussion, see Leon Gordenker, *The UN Secretary-General and the Maintenance of Peace* (New York: Columbia University Press, 1967), 152–156.

and unruly Congolese units were sometimes found outside of their country. Moreover, President Nyerere made no secret of his opposition to such leading Congolese politicians as Moïse Tshombe and General Mobutu. Ivan Smith's advice on such matters may have had some moderating influence on Tanzania's reactions to its neighbor's actions and was in any case heard.

In turn, Ivan Smith emphasized that his organization would do everything possible to meet Tanganyika's requests for development aid. Whenever such a request was made, sometimes only in a very tentative form, it was put into proper shape and transmitted to New York as quickly as possible, along with recommendations intended to speed its approval. This cooperative attitude was expected to reinforce Ivan Smith's ability to consult with the government on broader questions of Tanganyika's foreign policy and its activities in the United Nations, as well as to provide essential development services. Because Nyerere's government had pronounced and defined views as to its role in the United Nations and on the political development of southern and eastern Africa and because its leader lent his own prestige to his government's foreign policies, such consultations could conceivably have real importance as a source of information and support for the Secretary-General.

Although Ivan Smith did work closely with leading government figures in Tanganyika, it cannot be said that the technical assistance and preinvestment projects which were recommended by his office fitted together to form an articulated program. They did link with the national plan, but taken alone they had no pattern. Instead, they clearly were shaped in response to uncon-

69

nected requests from the government, rather than in response to stimulation and coordinated planning by the international agencies.

When Zambia became independent in 1964, Ivan Smith turned over his UNTAB and Special Fund duties in Dar es Salaam to a highly regarded Ghanaian, A. L. Adu, who had been head of the civil service in his own country and who was known throughout the English-speaking African colonies. Adu supervised what was still titled a regional program; in fact, it was three separate programs. A few projects involved all three countries or were to benefit the East African Community, which succeeded the administrative and operational arrangements established by the British colonial governments. He made no claim to political responsibilities, and his title was simply Regional Representative, rather than the more political Personal Representative of the Secretary-General. Nevertheless, Adu had easy access to political figures in Kenya and Uganda, as well as Tanzania, and was well informed about a broad range of government business.

Adu's experience in national administration and development programs, along with a marked proclivity for organizing, led him to seek a more interconnected international program in Tanzania than that with which he began. In such a program, each project would, as far as possible, reinforce every other. Resources would be concentrated in such a way as to make the best use of the talents of cooperating UN specialized agencies and to fit with maximum effect into the national plan. This organizational task was made easier as tentative requests from Tanzania began to exceed what it could expect to receive from the United Nations, thus giving Adu and his staff some opportunity to rank projects so as to produce a more coherent program. This activity required consultation with a greater range of government personnel than ever before and had the effect of widening the access that Ivan Smith had opened up.

Meanwhile, the regional concept, which had never been sharply defined, had decreasing meaning in the Dar es Salaam office. After Adu's resignation in 1966 to become Deputy Secretary-General of the Commonwealth, regional responsibilities were shifted to the UNDP office in Nairobi, thus reducing the points of access available in Tanzania. During this period also, Zanzibar was incorporated with Tanganyika in the United Republic of Tanzania; the Dar es Salaam office then became responsible for operations in Zanzibar and after much difficulty in clarifying its position on the island was able to continue a modest program. But operations in Zanzibar in effect had to be carried on with a government separate from that of the rest of the country, and much effort never yielded fully useful access.

At the same time, Ivan Smith began supervising another regional program from Lusaka, the Zambian capital. It covered Rhodesia, Bechuanaland, Basutoland, Swaziland, and, indirectly, Malawi. The relationship with the latter remained amorphous and contentious; the Resident Representatives in Malawi viewed their posts as largely autonomous of Lusaka. While Ivan Smith had direct supervision over all other programs, he had little more than copies of correspondence from Malawi. The programs in the other territories brought the Lusaka office into direct contact with the developing problem of Rhodesia's political future and, through the three British protectorates, with the problem of South Africa's resistance to UN pressure in opposition to apartheid. Whatever the rationale for a "regional"

71

economic program, Lusaka clearly offered a place from which to observe and to gain closer access to a developing and controversial political situation.

In this instance, as in Tanganyika earlier, the UN Secretary-General attached some importance to access to the top level of the new governments during the immediate postindependence stage. Ivan Smith therefore continued to use the title of Personal Representative and to carry out the observation and liaison duties that went with it. As in Tanzania, he developed relations with the political leaders of the government, giving special attention to President Kaunda, Foreign Minister Simon Kapepwe, and a few other highly influential leaders. His staff and technical assistance personnel also collected information about the ideas and plans of the government. Ivan Smith showed special interest in Zambian relations with Rhodesia and South Africa, and he found it possible to have talks with leading figures in Salisbury. The other independent government in his purview, Malawi, received much less attention, among other reasons because of difficulties in traveling to and communicating with Zomba.

Whether this access produced specific results in initiating and articulating UNTAB and Special Fund programs remains less than clear. Ivan Smith undertook his work when the experience with international organization programs in independent Zambia and Malawi was still new. The possibility of a unilateral declaration of independence by Rhodesia added an unpredictable and disturbing element but one which encouraged the United Nations to project a representation and liaison role beyond technical matters for its Resident Representative. In this atmosphere the priority given to political affairs by Ivan Smith seems to have strengthened the approval which international organization programs enjoyed in both cabinet and civil service circles. It helped to establish a general pattern of access to government which was useful to Ivan Smith's successors. One mark of this ease of access and general trust can be found in the fact that United Nations personnel were not included in the categories of foreign diplomats with whom Zambian civil servants could have only limited social contact by advance arrangement.

Ivan Smith's successors in both Tanzania and Zambia fitted more easily into the customary pattern of UNDP Resident Representatives,[8] emphasizing technical work and shunning overt interest in broader, especially security, policies. They kept closely informed on such general political developments as the effort to bring Zanzibar into a working relationship with Tanzania in the new United Republic or the deepening crisis induced by UDI and foreign responses to it. But the opportunity for their access to government officials arose primarily from aid problems, not those of more general international relations, and the Resident Representatives only occasionally used their access to discuss developments outside of their immediate impact on the aid program. One result of this course was that they directed their main consultative efforts to the top civil servants, rather than to ministers, and naturally showed much interest in the offices which coordinated and prepared government requests for foreign aid. Relationships with the planning activities of the governments, with finance and technical ministries, grew ever closer.

Some of the specialized agencies had their own rep-

[8] After Adu in Tanzania, Gertrude McKitterick, an American, who later returned to her former post at UNESCO; in Zambia, Richard Symonds and Anthony Gilpin, both British.

resentation for Malawi, Tanzania, and Zambia. These included ILO, UNESCO, FAO, and WHO. In addition, the UN Economic Commission for Africa had a sub-regional office in Lusaka; UNICEF, IBRD, the UN High Commissioner for Refugees, and the World Food Program were either represented by officials stationed in the countries or were near enough to visit as frequently as every month. Some of these officials worked closely with the Resident Representatives, as in the case of the World Food Program, which housed its officers in UNDP premises. But some agency officials kept aloof from the UNDP offices, sometimes as a matter of personal taste but more often in accordance with the practices of their institutions.

Representatives of specialized agencies deal with the top officials in the ministries whose work parallels their interests. They develop contacts on their own initiative, receiving orders not from the UNDP Resident Representative but from their own headquarters. Thus, the WHO representatives (one in Dar es Salaam and one in Lusaka, who also was responsible for Malawi) considered themselves advisers to the government on general matters of public health. They consulted frequently —sometimes on their own initiative and sometimes at the request of government personnel—with top officials and political heads. Their access was specialized but penetrated more deeply into the hierarchy than that of the Resident Representative. At the same time, representatives of the specialized agencies maintained a watch over the work of any technical assistance personnel or preinvestment projects in which their agency was involved. They offered advice to the UNDP Resident Representative on government requests for aid. Thus, their access to recipient governments did not depend on the presence or activities of the UNDP Resident Representative, but the work of both might be closely connected and mutually supporting.

In some instances the specialized agency representatives were incorporated directly into government structures in such a way as to guarantee effortless access to the concerned ministry. In Tanzania, for example, the chief of the FAO mission had also served for more than two years as a member of the planning unit in the Ministry of Agriculture, had directed long-term planning, and had been economic adviser to the minister. This arrangement (which was afterward abandoned in favor of experimenting with the use of the FAO representative as agricultural adviser to the Resident Representative) provided the international organization with constant access to the government activity with which it was most closely concerned. The ministry in turn had close access to the agency hierarchy.

A similar but looser arrangement evolved from the execution of the constitutional mandate of UNESCO for the formation of a national commission in each member country. A national commission is intended to assemble knowledgeable and influential people from within government and outside it to consider the national involvement with UNESCO. It is supposed to consult with the government and also, it is obvious, to function as a pressure group, favoring cooperation through UNESCO. Some official services have to be provided for such a commission. In Tanzania, the only country which had an officially established commission during the observation period, the Secretary-General of the Commission was a senior official in the Ministry of Education. Because he had inside knowledge of the ministry and kept himself informed on the more general

75

UNESCO program, he provided a natural point of contact for the agency's regional representative and staff in Dar es Salaam. UNESCO sent a representative to Zambia in 1966 (although he was later withdrawn). He immediately declared his intention to secure the establishment of a National Commission there as soon as possible. It was not clear, however, that an arrangement parallel to that in Tanzania ever came near establishment.

The National Commissions in the African countries under observation had a primarily ceremonial function. Persons with the kinds of knowledge and interests needed for successful work in such bodies were in such short supply and generally so fully occupied that they regarded the work of National Commissions as redundant of ministerial functions or superfluous. What was left, therefore, was a possibility for a UNESCO representative to develop a close working relationship with a ministry official. His participation on the commission merely indicated his particular specialization within the ministry: he was in effect the in-house expert on international educational cooperation.

In ambiguous and varying ways, technical assistance and OPEX personnel provide access for the permanent bureaucracies of the international organizations. Technical assistance experts by definition have short-term assignments and usually have no policy-making duties with regard to the organizations which recruit and deploy them. OPEX officials have duties equivalent to those of senior civil servants and are not responsible to the international organizations for their work; they are not required even to make a final report at the end of an assignment.

Of the two categories, the technical assistance personnel have the closer contact with their own agencies and with the Resident Representatives. They make periodic reports, which are transmitted through the Resident Representative; this alone assures some contact. At the end of a tour of duty, a technical assistance official also makes a final report, summing up his work and his recommendations. This report, submitted first to the agency involved and later officially transmitted to the government, also opens opportunities for access to decision-makers in the national governments. The international agencies attempt to couch reports in language which will not offend recipient governments and which will at the same time meet agency standards. It is usual for the government to see an early draft of the report, perhaps from the expert himself, and later from the agency to which it was transmitted, often with comments from the Resident Representative. Together the government and the agency decide whether the report should be published. All of this contact involves access to the government at several levels.

Similar contact arises, in principle, from the appointment and training of counterpart officials. These appointments, at least equaling the number of technical assistance experts, are considered a necessary part of the entire aid process and have particular importance in providing a means of transmitting the new techniques imported by the expatriate expert. Ideally, the appointment of a counterpart official should be made in close consultation with international agency personnel and should be an integral part of a program, rather than an afterthought. Some training of counterpart officials often takes place in institutes established by international agencies or in their headquarters. However, in the observed countries counterparts were sometimes not appointed at all. In other cases, poorly qualified officials who could be spared from work they performed indifferently were selected.

Expatriated and laboring under special conditions, all international personnel tend to develop a certain feeling of kinship with others in their status. The household problems of living in a strange land affect all of them, and many of them, moreover, know each other from other assignments. Especially in the capitals, they usually remain in close and friendly touch with each other. Through this means, OPEX personnel also provide a certain quality of access to the decision process.

OPEX and technical assistance experts have often held crucial positions within the political process of putting forward requests for further assistance. Sometimes these positions were held at the very early stage of working up and executing the national development plan. For example, the United Nations furnished Economic Advisers to the governments of Malawi and Zambia during part of the observation period. The mere fact that these people were recruited and paid for by the United Nations tended to open direct access for the Resident Representatives. Because these officials had duties that involved the entire national planning process, access to them was especially interesting. It provided information about and perhaps considerable influence on the requests that led to continuing involvement of the international organizations.

In addition to the access established by international organization personnel to the officials of the governments receiving aid, international organizations obtain access in two ways from the outside. First, almost all of the organizations customarily send visiting missions of varying size and distinction to the receiving countries.

Second, governments participate in international conferences dealing with a wide range of subject matter in a variety of institutional settings.

In some instances, the three observed governments have requested visits by specialized personnel from international agencies. Some of these visitors appear for only brief consultations, perhaps as short as a day or two, on a narrowly defined subject, e.g., generation of useful trade statistics. Or, consultants may be summoned to help with the definition and drafting of a request for assistance. The IBRD, for example, sent several missions to the area. One of them attracted much diplomatic attention with its task of advising on the economic feasibility of a railway from Zambia to the Tanzanian coast. This controversial project grew directly out of Tanzanian and Zambian policies of keeping pressure on Rhodesia, in an attempt to ward off a declaration of independence, and of freeing the whole region of economic interdependence with South Africa and the Portuguese colonies. Similarly, advisers on such specialized problems as trade promotion or statistical services are available for short-term assignments from the UN Economic Commission for Africa and were requested occasionally by the governments of the three countries.

The Resident Representatives were not always involved in developing requests for these short-term missions. In some instances, they learned of the arrival of an adviser only by chance. This kind of incident clearly shows that access is not identical with full coordination of international programs.

Frequently—more frequently than local representatives sometimes enjoy and approve—visiting missions grow out of initiatives at international organization

79

headquarters. The IBRD, for example, periodically makes comprehensive economic surveys of East Africa, including one during the period of observation. These surveys, which are kept confidential, primarily inform the bank staff, but findings are also put before the governments. The reports invariably are described as frank and critical, but the fact that the governments see all or part of them is known to induce a certain delicacy in drafting.

IBRD officials not only consult governmental officials but also a variety of influential private persons in banks and other businesses. The resulting surveys are taken seriously by member governments and private persons because of the possibility that consideration of later loan applications will be influenced by the findings. Moreover, the governments also hope that the reports will identify development possibilities suitable for future investment by means of IBRD loans. These missions, always referred to as "high-powered," have almost unlimited access to government servants and to political leaders. Such access is precisely what is intended by the IBRD. The Resident Representative on the spot has little influence over them and can control neither their schedules nor their progress. During the observation period, the IBRD missions at first took little account of the UNDP, but increasing cooperation was noted. Yet it does not seem that the Resident Representative was always fully informed of conversations held by IBRD representatives; he sometimes learned of conclusions only much later by indirect routes.

Most survey missions, however "high-powered," have a more limited scope and include only two or three officials, in contrast to more than fifteen on the IBRD team. The UNDP, for example, sent small missions headed by such high officials as Paul-Marc Henry, then an Assistant Administrator with deep knowledge of Africa, or Lord Caradon, former permanent representative of the United Kingdom to the United Nations and also an expert on Africa.

Some missions receive less than enthusiastic welcomes by member governments, whose few capable civil servants have to contend with complicated and exhausting agendas. In Malawi, for example, nine successive visits within the space of three months were scheduled by one agency, with the result that the weary bureaucracy insisted on tightening its procedures for permission to visit. The ministers, and especially the civil servants concerned, believed they simply had to husband their time and that the international agencies could operate in closer coordination and employ the services of the Resident Representative to better effect.

The same national ministers and officials who receive visitors from agencies often represent their governments in their specialized fields at general and technical international meetings. The Minister of Agriculture and chief officials, for example, usually make up delegations to the FAO Conference and other meetings. There they encounter international civil servants who but a few weeks earlier had conferred with them in their own countries. In a few instances, the delegation was known to have consulted international agency representatives in their own capital with regard to the subjects likely to be discussed at the meeting and the position they should hold. Such participation of international officials in briefing delegations did not, however, appear to be common practice during the observation period.

On a few occasions of considerable importance, officials supplied by international agencies were included as members of national delegations to international meetings. Mutual access of agencies and member governments could hardly be better than this, but this practice clearly was exceptional. It does, however, demonstrate a highly trusting relationship between the government and international personnel concerned.

International conferences themselves provide access of a different sort to national decision-makers. National representatives necessarily must react to policy proposals and plans that emerge from the meetings. These are framed more broadly than those of their own governments. Since such policies more often than not are formulated by the secretariats of international agencies, the reactions of government representatives provide important clues to the specific nature of projects which are likely to be acceptable. International meetings therefore encourage the creation of access routes from national government personnel to the headquarters establishments of the international agencies.[9] At the same time, conferences provide opportunities for informal talks during which specific national problems can be reviewed and discussed, sometimes at the initiative of international officials and in the privacy of their offices. Access based on the active and often impressive setting of international conferences may thus have an important bearing on the kind of atmosphere that exists at

---

[9] Cox and Jacobson, *Anatomy of Influence*, provides information about the various roles of the secretariats in some of the agencies involved in the UNDP and their aid programs. By differentiating between symbolic and service functions of the agencies, they make it clear that the secretariats play a determinating role in the latter, which include field operations. See also their useful distinctions of country, representative, and participant subsystems, pp. 16–17.

the national level for the initiation and execution of specific projects.

Official programs and relationships often—perhaps usually—create their informal counterpart. Senior international personnel visiting or working in recipient countries receive invitations to diplomatic and government parties and receptions. They usually try to return the hospitality, especially that of government leaders. In this milieu, relaxed, less defined conversation can supplement more businesslike relationships. Moreover, both senior and junior officials usually develop some friendships, or at least understanding acquaintances, with their working colleagues and thus form another access route. But friendship does not develop automatically and can be impeded by numerous obstacles that support personal animosities, which not infrequently can be found. Such emnities, centering on the work or the personality of an international official, sometimes spread throughout the government structure, reducing ease of access and destroying the effect of informal contacts.

Multiple Access and Interpenetration

The formal structures created for the administration of international aid programs and their counterparts within national governments offer a remarkable number of opportunities for mutual access. The international civil servants representing international agencies had a wide range of contacts within the governments of the observed countries. The national governments had access to the international policy process in numerous ways.

Criss-crossing patterns of access were sometimes

formed, allowing national and international civil servants to trade views and share work at every level of the aid process. Internationally furnished personnel, working with national officials, had access at an early stage to the information and discussions that led eventually to requests for aid or to alteration or discontinuation of a project underway. Whatever use they made of it, national officials and political leaders had access to the policy-making process in international agencies. The great variety of access routes and the presence of international personnel in several capacities within the national bureaucracies led to routine, accepted, and pervasive interpenetration.

The criss-crossing patterns of access may be thought of as interpenetration, actual and potential, of the legally separate international and national hierarchies of decision-makers. Mutual access is neither constant nor regular, but it is always present and in practice. It is characteristic of the process of field operations and also the ladder to influence on policy at higher levels of international organization structures.

In addition to mutual access among formal decision-making agencies, a network of informal relationships, too tangled to be traced here but nevertheless obvious to an observer, are fostered by the comings and goings of participants to international organization meetings and by the visits of headquarters personnel. In this way a vast amount of information accumulates over time and to some extent provides a common basis for the progress of international programs and national development. How the common modes of operation are determined and how the programs come into being will be discussed further in the next chapter.

3.

INFLUENCE: PROJECTS

THE operations of the administrative structures in international agencies and those of governments receiving aid helps to establish a process of mutual influence. Elements of this influence process relate to specific development projects that receive international support. Such projects vary greatly in subject matter and in degree of involvement by international agencies and governments. It would be impossible to develop a general statement of this influence process so as to give specific weight to each example of development projects. Yet some insights into the process and its operation may be found in specific case material. This chapter will use examples from Tanzania, Malawi, and Zambia to show how the influence process bears on and develops from the initiation of projects and the changing of their dimensions. The next chapter will examine how advice is conveyed to the top level of governments and how field operations of international agencies respond to political crises.

INITIATING A REQUEST: ZAMBIA

One cool, starlit evening during the southern African summer of early 1966, the conversation around a campfire in the Luangwa game reserve in eastern Zambia had a far more serious tone than the usual comments of animal-watching tourists. It dealt with the possibility of technical studies to safeguard and guide the future of the game park, the animals in it, and the land and people of the river valley in which it was located.

One of the group was then head of the game department of the Zambian government, a biologist who had spent a decade nurturing the game parks, which could become valuable tourist assets. He expressed fear that the vast, isolated Luangwa Valley and the two national parks in it faced degradation and ruin as places of natural beauty. Numerous elephants, some in herds of more than one hundred, and the milling thousands of Cape buffalo were eating themselves and the valley into a decline. Hippopotami wandered from the river to add to the destruction of the land flora. The game expert urged use of sophisticated techniques to reduce the animal population before nothing was left. To that end, he had already begun to seek outside aid and had in mind studies that the UNDP could sponsor and the FAO could execute to help in planning the future of Luangwa Valley.

Another member of the group around the campfire was a project officer of the UNDP Regional Representative's office in Lusaka. Various officials of the game department had discussed with her the Luangwa Valley and its problems repeatedly during the previous several months. She had accumulated considerable knowledge of the situation there. Both she and the game department head agreed that the troubles in the Luangwa parks had caused wider problems than the mere overpopulation of game. As elsewhere in Africa, expanding human occupation of land had crowded the animals out, forcing them into ranges too small for their numbers. At the headwaters of the Luangwa River, which drains into the Zambezi and thus connects with Mozambique, peasant farmers each year enlarged the cultivated area, digging new plots out of the bush and stripping the soil of protective vegetation. As a result, it was thought, floods down the valley reached higher levels each year, the soil-stained red waters streaming over the poor fields of local farmers and biting into the land of the parks.

The UNDP project officer, along with some of the officials in the Zambian planning ministry whom she had informally consulted, viewed the Luangwa Valley problem as implying yet larger issues of economic development. The game department, too, considered its more specialized proposals for conservation and tourism to be tied to general economic planning. Established under the colonial government, with perhaps little enthusiasm from local people, the national park now was a valuable asset to the economic development of Zambia. It could draw thousands of tourists, as parks in Kenya and Tanzania did, creating jobs and funneling foreign exchange into the country. It needed larger and better hotels and camps and easier access from Lusaka, where international flights landed. But it would be worthless to consider, let alone to provide capital for an area that was on an unchecked or irreversible decline. At the same time, the farmers at the head of the valley and the few who lived along the edges of the park on the lower river also had needs and rights. They did not break into the virgin land merely because it was there, but rather because the population was growing; in some nearby districts, the fragile soil had failed under the pressure of steady production, poor protection, and uneven rainfall. But if the valley could be treated as a unit for planning, many interests might benefit and disruption of human life and the environment could be reduced.

The game department had already experimented with several notions intended to serve multiple interests, beginning with a pilot project for game cropping. Rangers armed with rifles that fired poison-injecting devices slaughtered small numbers of elephant, hippopotamus, and buffalo. With tractors, they dragged the heavy carcasses to a factory where the meat of the animals was frozen or dried for use as human food and the hides and ivory prepared for sale. It was thought that meat from surplus game could be delivered in considerable quantities at a price lower than meat from domestic animals. In any case, meat was much in demand in the capital and the larger towns in the Copper Belt, where relatively well-paid workers could afford it. Reduction of the animal population, it was hoped, would not only improve the quality of the herds but would also take some of the pressure off the land.

Yet this pilot project had hardly done more than to underscore the questions. What was surplus game? How much game should be taken to protect the future of the herds and of the dependent tourist industry? How acceptable was the processed meat of wild game animals to workers in the cities and mining towns? Did it run counter to their tastes or even to tribal taboos? What new transportation would be needed for access to and within the valley? Would more tourist accommodation be required? What would it do to the ecology of the valley? How much farming could be permitted without upsetting the ecological scheme of the lower valley and perhaps of the Zambezi as well? What alternative development schemes could be devised and what would they cost?

Such questions had an obvious relationship to economic development, either in furnishing the required data for more precise planning or involving formulation of a practical program. They were implicitly accepted by the project officer as falling within the flexible guidelines set by the UNDP. Their relevance to the national plan, a preliminary question raised by the UNDP in all applications for assistance, was clear. The plan then in existence emphasized the development of tourism, agriculture, and the welfare of urban workers as goals. A new national plan had not yet reached the drafting stage, but the UNDP office had some information on its likely contents. Negotiations were about to be concluded for the appointment of a planning chief under the OPEX scheme; the UNDP office had helped with some aspects of the appointment and some of its personnel knew the official who was to be appointed. If the UNDP reacted quickly, specific goals for the Luangwa Valley and the possible role for international aid might be written into the new plan.

The campfire discussion had been preceded by considerable preparation in the machinery of the UN system. Concern with the Luangwa Valley had already led officials of the Ministry of Agriculture, Forestry, and Fisheries to approach the FAO about the possibility of some expert assistance for projects in the valley. This approach had apparently been made independently of the UNDP structure. Instead, it went through conventional contacts between the international organization and the ministry and was intended mainly to collect information about the possibility of help. The response from the FAO was simultaneously enthusiastic, disappointing, and typical.

Letters from FAO headquarters in Rome supported an inquiry into the ecology of the valley. This would be an excellent project, because it would obviously pro-

89

vide understanding about an important part of Zambia; it was connected with development, might produce new knowledge, and was well within the range of projects that the secretariat of the organization thought should be supported. Zambian officials received encouragement, even if it were limited to expressions of moral support. The FAO suggested that a survey of the Luangwa Valley would make a fine project for the Special Fund division of the UNDP. The FAO could offer no direct financial help but only encouragement and backing if the Zambian government were to decide to apply to the UNDP. By encouragement and backing, the FAO meant that its officials would advise on the application, would urge the UNDP to approve the project, and would prepare for the execution of the survey, logically an affair for the FAO to supervise.

However disappointing this response may have been for national officials, who perhaps naively hoped that they could quickly get their ideas off paper and into the field with international help, it was typical of the aid process at this stage. The approach by the agriculture ministry flowed along normal lines. The national civil servants, many of them still expatriates, thought of international aid as a way to extend national financing. They knew something of the FAO, and some of them had participated in one or another conference convened by the organization. Some knew members of the international secretariat. To appeal to the FAO seemed obvious to agriculture department officials, who had less knowledge at that time of the UNDP, even if it were locally represented. The UNDP was after all a bureaucratic channel used by another department and was therefore less prominent in the minds of the agriculture ministry officials.

As for the FAO, it had practically no funds of its own for development purposes. It receives such financing from the UNDP on the basis of approved projects. The idea of a survey of the Luangwa Valley fell within the range of what one division of FAO considered its mission, for it related to increasing the productivity of wildlife and forestry and to protecting the land. It therefore encouraged Zambia to approach the UNDP. If successful, this application would further the FAO program generally and the work of an FAO division, as its personnel conceived it, in particular. In practice, it would mean that the FAO would execute the Luangwa project, appointing the personnel, supervising their work, and taking some credit for success.

The next step in developing a request for assistance through international channels then involved the UNDP. Another option was to turn away from the international agencies altogether and to seek help from a government which operated its own program, such as the United Kingdom or the Netherlands. (The United States, sometimes thought of as the biggest donor, was at this time consolidating its African programs in countries other than Zambia.) A third option was to finance the Luangwa study entirely from Zambian funds, but this had tacitly been rejected when the FAO was approached. It appears that the correspondence with the FAO had led Zambian officials to prefer international channels (or tacitly to reject bilateral support), and a meeting was set up with UNDP representatives in Lusaka late in 1965.

In the course of a conversation at the UNDP office, during which the chief game officer, an Assistant Resident Representative who in effect directed the program for Zambia, and the project officer reviewed what had

91

been done so far. It soon developed that whatever followed would depend on whether a Special Fund project should be the aim of the request. By its nature, a Special Fund project involves much complexity of decision: it is intended to go into enough depth to provide a basis for substantial investment and is expected to handle a development project in a comprehensive manner; the number of personnel is likely to be large in comparison with one-, two-, or three-member technical assistance advisory teams; the duration of the project would be from three to five years; and, finally, it would require matching funds from the Zambian government totaling perhaps several hundred thousand dollars. To seek such a project obviously would involve some careful planning and the cementing of relationships among several government departments and within the cabinet itself.

The UNDP officials, moreover, pointed out that a Special Fund project would involve considerable delay, because requests now pending from the Zambian government had already exceeded the target figure. This latter was the guideline made up in New York on the basis of advice from the Resident Representative, expected resources, size of continuing programs, and any other factors which might seem important, such as equity of allocations among countries and expectations as to the amount of aid that could be absorbed easily in any economy. This system of country guidelines has since been abandoned, but whatever the basis for planning for distribution of UNDP resources, the same sorts of questions are involved. No rational means of selecting donor targets can be found in the presence of such imponderables as equity and ability to digest aid. The decisions therefore can be placed in the category of political, rather than technical, choices.

92

One Zambian official passionately interested in the project, which he was convinced had great possibilities for development and for professional research, wanted to continue the work in progress on game cropping and to widen its implications. He pressed for some kind of international aid that could quickly accomplish at least this much. This conversation indicated to UNDP personnel a degree of commitment on the part of appropriate technical officials in the Zambian government that promised a favorable attitude toward almost any relevant proposals which might be made. After some discussion in the UNDP office, the project officer suggested to the game department head that it might be possible to begin some studies almost immediately by applying to the UNDP for an allocation from the Contingency Fund, the 10 percent of the annual budget which was directly controlled by the Executive Director. A decision could be obtained quickly on whether financing would be available. Whether an eventual request for a much larger Special Fund project should be made, it was suggested, would depend on the outcome of further study under the leadership of the technical assistance experts supported by the UNDP and recruited by the FAO. Such study could develop data and arguments for a Special Fund project or, alternatively, could demonstrate its futility. The Zambian administration could be informed more fully about the possibilities for a Special Fund project, and any future decisions could be well prepared.

This procedure received quick approval from the head of the game department. The UNDP officials specifically suggested that an official request should be made for two experienced consultants on problems of range management. The consultants would work for

93

one year, two at most, on studies of the Luangwa Valley. Their salaries could be paid for, it was thought, out of the Contingency Fund, while the Zambian government would be responsible for the usual local costs, such as transportation and suitable housing. At this point, the project officer was invited by the game department to visit the Luangwa Valley for a first-hand impression of the situation there. The possible benefits of such a visit seemed clear, but it was also a spectacular pleasure to be conducted around the game reserve by the experienced game wardens and to be flown over the entire area in the light aircraft used by the wardens to keep track of the herds.

During the next few weeks, a request for UNDP technical assistance was worked up in proper form. Officially, the Zambian government had responsibility for the request. Informally, UNDP officials played a major role. Their advice and recommendations were constantly available and more than once offered on individual initiative; some parts of the request were drafted in the UNDP office. Aid coordinators in the planning office of the Zambian government also came into the discussions. Their eventual approval of the project would be needed, and in any case theirs was the only Zambian agency empowered to forward a request. During this time, the Regional Representative had had at least two exchanges of correspondence with his New York headquarters before forwarding an official document with his favorable endorsement. The FAO had also been kept informed of the preparation of the request. Immediately after approval of the project in New York, the FAO began the process of recruiting the two experts, one a wildlife biologist and the other a wildlife ecologist. The two chosen from a short list drawn up by the FAO and put before the Zambian government came from the United States, where they had had experience in range management and research for the American government. Both were at work in the Luangwa Valley by the end of 1966. Some veteran UNDP officials remarked then that the process of recruitment and appointment had taken less than the usual time, thus reflecting their concern with the UNDP's reputation for slow decision-making.

From the beginning of the contacts between Zambian civil servants and the FAO more than a year preceding the arrival of the two experts, both sides had intended to decide whether a major development survey of the valley should be undertaken. The Zambian civil servants had little doubt as to its desirability, although the UNDP officials welcomed a chance to accumulate more information and experience with the problem before endorsing an application. It was not clear at the outset that the application would receive endorsement at the ministerial level, which was necessary in view of the likely size of the government's contribution. The UNDP officials had no reason, however, to think that the idea would be rejected out of hand once it reached the ministerial level.

As is usual in such situations, competition within the government put a premium on good preparation of the project, convincing argument about it, and solidarity within the ministry concerned. It was hoped by both the Zambian civil servants and the UNDP that the work of the two experts had helped to promote within the ministry a common goal of securing international aid. The experts themselves were a sign that agencies outside Zambia would seriously be interested, and Zambia could argue, probably with support from the Regional

Representative, that a Special Fund application had been well prepared.

In fact, an application for a Special Fund project was formulated during 1967 and 1968 and sent to New York. As in the case of the request for the two technical assistance experts, the same process of discussion, drafting, and cross-checking between the ministry and the UNDP, and clearing through the government aid coordination agency took place. In spite of doubt about approval at the ministerial level, the application was endorsed by the Zambian government in 1968, when it was formally approved by the UNDP. The project was to begin in 1969.

As had been envisaged from the earliest conversations, the project's general survey and research purposes fell well within Special Fund practices. Its aim was to develop natural resources and improve conservation of wildlife as well as to promote tourism. Definite plans along these lines could eventually attract substantial investment or become the basis of a loan application to the International Bank or other sources. The FAO was named as the executing agency, fulfilling the purposes that its officials had had in mind from the first. The project's budget was $3.7 million, with the government contributing $2.6 million in the form of counterpart personnel, offices, equipment, and supporting staff. The project officially began in June 1969, when a project manager started work. Beyond his appointment was another series of consultations, involving the UNDP, the FAO, other agencies, and the government. Staff needed to be recruited, and the actual field survey and research had to be organized.

Although it was not possible to observe later developments in the project, its creation was on the whole smooth and direct. From the beginning, its purpose had been sharply defined. The Zambian official charged with carrying it along stayed with the project so that it was not affected by changing personnel. The project was easy to defend as consonant with the Zambian development plan. It had been the subject of modest experiments and could be easily understood from both technical and lay standpoints. The international machinery was efficiently used to plan further employment and expansion of support from the UN system. The government machinery meshed almost faultlessly with its United Nations counterpart, partly because of good understanding and personal sympathy among the national and international officials concerned, partly because the Resident Representatives concerned thought the project a useful one. No competition among agencies in the UN system emerged, perhaps because the idea so readily fell within the jurisdiction of the FAO, and there within a division that had done work along similar lines elsewhere. Some of the facility with which the project took shape could be laid to fortuitous factors. In its early stages the project did not get caught up in intragovernmental competition, although later information that the Chief Game Officer had been dismissed pointed to the possibility of a policy change that might affect the Luangwa Valley survey.

SHAPING PROJECT DIMENSIONS: TANZANIA

Giving definition to a request for international aid can lead to considerable friction within and among the organizations of the UN system as well as to divisions of opinion within the recipient government. Intractable disagreements can prevent the submission of a request.

Even if a formula can be found, the original idea for the project is likely to undergo marked alteration.

Evidence of such disagreement is easily encountered in a field setting, although piecing together the full story of any incident more often than not proves difficult. This discussion therefore will suffer from the effects of bureaucratic restraint in both national and international administrations. Generally speaking, neither national nor international civil servants were anxious to parade before an outsider their problems of finding agreement. More positively seen, they generally followed their training and tried to find compromise solutions to problems that developed from viewing the same proposal from different standpoints. It is at the technical level that differences may most clearly emerge, because the work of experts at that level implies the attempt to define issues. At the more general level of the cabinet or the head of government, the details of a proposed request for aid or the direction and aims of a preinvestment program are likely to be buried under more general political considerations, such as the sharing out of scarce foreign exchange resources among ministries whose heads have political debts to deal with. It is not inconceivable that an internationally aided development project could become the focus of a broad political conflict in a recipient government. Some proposals can threaten to upset decisions as to the nature of development efforts, while others can distort development plans by giving special emphasis to one sector without regard to the effects on another. In political terms, a development project can easily cause conflicts that require mediation at the cabinet level or can result in involvement by the head of government.

A proposal for a survey of river valleys in Tanganyika (at that time not yet Tanzania) concretely illustrates many of the outcomes that a more abstract scenario would lead an observer to expect. This project began to emerge in late 1961, when Tanganyika had not yet attained independence, and it was defined and redefined several times over the next four years. A number of conflicts and their successful resolution can be documented. Meanwhile, the Tanzanian government elaborated its own approach to development, with relatively little reliance on the suppositions of international agencies. President Julius Nyerere consequently acquired an international reputation and respect as a statesman. The proposed river valleys survey thus bridged the end of the colonial period and the beginning of independence, and also preceded the radical redefinition in the Arusha Declaration of the Tanzanian's approach to economic development. Precisely because the Arusha Declaration represents an unusual approach, which has not been imitated, reflections on the river valleys survey may have more general application outside Tanzania than some of the later projects in that country. Nevertheless, the ability of the international agencies to continue working within the framework of the Arusha program should not be overlooked. If consideration of the river valleys survey exhibits some rigidity in the operations of international agencies, the post-Arusha period in Tanzania indicates that they can also employ their resources with considerable flexibility.

The river surveys project developed through a series of phases, each of which involved a conflict within the UN structure and a reaction from the government. These phases may be described as follows: (1) suggestion by the FAO; (2) definition of the role of the Special

Fund; (3) redefinition within the government; (4) critical reaction by the Special Fund; (5) conflict between the Special Fund and the government, with intervention by the FAO; (6) high-level mediation from Special Fund officials; (7) redefinition of the project and agreement on a plan of operations. The eventual agreement was never a foregone conclusion and represents the outcome of strong pressures on the part of the Tanzanian government, the Special Fund, the FAO, and several advisory officials.

The FAO's original suggestion involved an irrigation survey of the Pangani (Ruvu) and Rufiji areas under Special Fund auspices. As is so often the case in development projects, the precise source of the idea cannot now be traced. The colonial government had done some survey work related to river valley development, but this had not led to large-scale projects or even to the accumulation of files complete enough for planning by later specialists. In mid-1961, Paul Bomani, an old friend and associate of President Nyerere and then Minister of Finance, visited Rome and discussed possible programs for his country with the FAO. Officials of the Land and Water Development Division of the FAO talked with him about a preinvestment survey of the Pangani and Rufiji areas. Sometime afterward, the FAO Director-General wrote to the Tanganyikan government, submitting a draft application for a Special Fund project.

When in October this proposal came, accidentally, to the attention of the Resident Representative's office in Dar es Salaam,[1] an immediate protest at being by-

---

[1] At this time, the field offices of the UNTAB were headed by Resident Representatives who also were titled Director of the UN Special Fund program in each country. The two organi-

passed was dispatched to the FAO, which explained that the draft was preliminary and for the comment of the government only. Minor issues developed throughout the negotiations. The government did not accept the FAO draft at first, pointing out that local costs were too high and that the development of the Rufiji basin in any case conflicted with present development planning policy. By this time, the Resident Representative had become a partner in the discussions.

Hesitation by the government could have killed the entire project, but the arrival of a team of French government experts charged with seeking possible projects related to river development,[2] and the presence of an FAO irrigation engineer advising the government, helped to keep the idea alive. Within the Ministry of Agriculture some senior civil servants, at that time almost all expatriates, also showed interest in the idea of a preinvestment survey. Questions and contacts with the Special Fund office kept this interest at a high level. It resulted in another discussion in Rome between the FAO and the Minister of Agriculture, D. M. Bryceson, a European who, as a Tanzanian national, continued in his post after independence. By mid-May 1962, the original draft for the Pangani and Rufiji areas had been revised and put in the hands of the government and of the Special Fund office in Dar es Salaam. By this time, then, the Special Fund had fully established an interest at the field level, the FAO had created a work-

---

zations were formally separated at headquarters, although they increasingly worked closely together. For the sake of simplicity, the title Resident Representative will be used here.

[2] The ranking expatriate planner in Dar es Salaam and principal author of the development plan then in force was a French national.

ing relationship with the Ministry of Agriculture, and within the FAO a group of officials had committed considerable time and effort to creating a project which would be accepted by both the government and the Special Fund.

The formal request by the government was not submitted to the Special Fund representative in Dar es Salaam, George Ivan Smith, until early September 1962. Between then and May 1963, both the international and national officials in Dar es Salaam and the FAO group in Rome had further committed themselves to the survey project. Both Bryceson and Bomani, accompanied by senior officials, had visited Rome for further discussions; an important FAO official had come to Dar es Salaam; and Ivan Smith had discussed the May draft again in Rome and found support from the FAO. The government sought assistance in investigating the further development of irrigation in the Pangani and Rufiji valleys, which represented two river systems separated by several hundred miles and having origins in different sections of the Tanzanian mountains. The application was covered by a letter which noted the work already done by the FAO in the basins and stated that the government considered the project of great importance in increasing productivity and raising living standards. At the same time, the government noted that it could not meet its 70 percent share of the cost of the project—30 percent being the Special Fund's contribution—and that it would approach outside sources for help.

Formal submission of the request to UN Special Fund headquarters in New York produced procedural delays and serious questions about the project itself. The September date was two months past the deadline for application to the January 1963 session of the Governing Council, which makes final decisions. Furthermore, the government's letter referred to a draft program, which caused the operations director in New York to query Dar es Salaam for a clarification. The procedural delays provided time for the Special Fund to raise questions of substance with the FAO, and these provoked some serious reactions.

Although the Special Fund headquarters staff thought in general that the request would be accepted by the Governing Council, which meant that it would have an endorsement from the staff as well as from the field office, enough defects were found to warrant the suggestion that an FAO expert be sent to reformulate the proposal. One of the defects ran directly counter to Special Fund policy: no commitment but only a hope was expressed to provide counterpart personnel. More serious was uncertainty about how extensive a program was envisaged as an outcome of the preinvestment survey. The cost of developing only 1.5 million acres in the Rufiji basin was estimated at $390 million, a figure far out of reach for Tanganyika. Over ten years the cost estimate was set at $77 million for both rivers, raising the question of what exactly was going to be done and when and where. In effect, then, the Special Fund indicated that some clarifications would leave the request ripe for action at the May 1963 meeting of the Governing Council.

The outcome in Dar es Salaam had anything but exclusively technical overtones. Rather, the letter from New York set off a series of actions within the government that produced a proposal with a different perspective. This proposal was based in considerable part on expert advice from the Ministry of Agriculture's economic adviser, who was himself an FAO official.

Ivan Smith's reports to the Special Fund on the reaction in the government to the criticism of the Pangani-Rufiji scheme emphasized political factors. Tanganyika would become independent within a few weeks; President Nyerere wanted practical programs of broad effect and emphasized early results rather than fuller research; orderly development for the future should be undertaken within the limits of available local resources and without the distortions implicit in certain bilateral offers already received by the government. He also suggested that the International Bank should be associated with the eventual project, apparently in order to keep it continuously informed of investment possibilities.

Within the Ministry of Agriculture, the FAO economics adviser, who had recently come on the scene and had just been asked for his advice, strongly criticized the proposal in the hands of the Special Fund. It represented in part, he indicated, a fixed professional notion of the entrenched irrigation specialists within Tanganyika and the FAO. It had insufficient provision for soil surveys and thus could not possibly persuade future investors of its worth. Other agricultural factors were pushed aside in favor of water engineering. Existent surveys gave enough information; no new grandiose survey was needed. The Special Fund failed to take into account the almost insuperable difficulties in providing counterpart funds. He urged that any consultant sent to Tanganyika to review the proposal should have wider interests than irrigation and water development, and the World Bank should be brought into the work. With fast action, he believed, a new proposal could be submitted in time to meet the deadline for the May 1963 meeting of the Governing Council. He reported in a similar vein to both Ivan Smith and Bryceson.

The FAO sent a water resources consultant to Dar es Salaam, and, with the cooperation of the FAO economics adviser and Ministry of Agriculture officials, a substitute document was readied by late November. It was in effect a new proposal, turned out in record time. Instead of concentrating on irrigation and water development surveys in the Rufiji and Pangani valleys, five river basins were selected for their potential for effective and quick demonstration of land settlement, irrigation projects, and use of existing survey data. The new plan received consideration at the cabinet level and close attention from Nyerere, who saw in it a chance to begin something practical and orderly. Ivan Smith thought that the President attached much importance to the new scheme, and both FAO advisers judged it practical, useful, and well-founded.

The reaction at FAO headquarters could be read as confirming the FAO economic adviser's warning against rigid approaches by entrenched groups. It was based on a conversation with Special Fund officials, who were said to view the new proposal as a countrywide survey, which was ruled out as an acceptable category of pre-investment projects. FAO headquarters thought that if the government could be induced to go back to the original draft, the project would probably be approved at the next meeting of the Governing Council. The clear intimation was that any other project would have to wait for an indefinite period. A new draft, prepared with the help of the consultant who had been in Tanganyika, returned to the concept of the Pangani and Ruvu river valleys as the center of a survey which now

105

would have additional pilot project elements. Rejection of the five river proposal by the engineering branch of the Special Fund apparently increased the impetus behind the new approach.

However, the new approach promptly turned the Special Fund representative, the Minister of Agriculture, and the FAO economic adviser into a solid front of opposition to the decisions in New York and Rome. It also resulted in a delay of the entire project until after the May meeting of the Governing Council. An extended correspondence by letter and cable, involving New York and Rome, followed, beginning with the news that the Minister of Agriculture opposed the return to the two rivers approach and insisted that the rejected proposal had been just what the government wanted in the way of demonstration projects in areas capable of early development. The scheme had top priority, he was quoted as saying, and if the UN system could not help, other sources might.

On the basis of reports to Bryceson by Ivan Smith's Dar es Salaam office, the minister protested that Tanganyika was being unfairly treated and that his government should have had some say in whether or not its own project would be accepted. He implied that by returning to the original FAO idea the Special Fund had rejected informed advice in favor of insufficient study, and he insisted that the project was practical, sound, and in line with the government's policy of development. His challenge to the Special Fund listed five complaints: the policy was too narrow; local conditions should be taken into account; any doubts about the suitability of the proposal should have been resolved by the Governing Council, not the staff; the Special Fund had no authority to question the Tanganyika development plan; and study of the proposal was not competent and objective.

This was a far-reaching challenge to both policies and procedures of the Special Fund headquarters. It came when the Special Fund was eager to build up its work in Africa and when the first of the East African governments was reaching independence. The protest also tended to squeeze the Special Fund personnel in Dar es Salaam between two views. If they supported the government, as they tended to do, their enthusiasm could diminish their influence in New York. If they did not support the government, their effectiveness in Dar es Salaam would be sapped. In short, the level of discussion had been raised from technical to political.[3]

Ivan Smith cabled from New York that both the government and international sides misunderstood the situation. The Dar es Salaam office should withhold any action while a top level meeting was held at Special Fund headquarters. His office then wrote to President Nyerere, informing him of Ivan Smith's advice that no decisive action be taken until the whole matter had been reconsidered. Ivan Smith wanted the President to know that the Special Fund was interested in and sympathetic with the project. Meanwhile, in New York, Ivan Smith urged that a top level representative be sent to try to straighten out the matter, and he continued to advocate that on his return.

In Dar es Salaam, Ivan Smith found the government prepared to listen, and he secured from the Special

---

[3] A technical issue can be defined as one posed entirely within an agreed project framework. A political question involves questions of authority, choices of procedure, and definitions of the boundaries of a project in which the national government takes a position that doubts or opposes that of the international organization.

Fund the commitment of a high-level visit, which was carried out by Roberto Huertematte, the Deputy Administrator. In the course of his discussions, it appeared that the comments from New York had been taken by the government as an irrevocable criticism. In fact, they had apparently been intended as an internal document which would make possible further discussion between the Special Fund and the government. Once the Special Fund had demonstrated its sympathy with the Tanganyikan aims, it became possible for the Special Fund officials in the Dar es Salaam office to work with the FAO economic adviser, who had the full trust of the minister, on revising the proposal for the survey of the five river valleys. The Special Fund official in charge pleaded for a smaller and more specific project which might have demonstration effects for other valleys, rather than an undertaking which would be spread thin. This approach produced an agreement to reformulate the entire request.

During June 1964, a senior official of the Land and Water Development Division of the FAO joined the economic adviser and Special Fund personnel in Dar es Salaam to consult with the Ministry of Agriculture on the reformulation. The main burden of the revision was carried by the international officials, who reached agreement with the Minister that the five river project should indeed be trimmed back to two. But now the Wami River was substituted for the Ruvu, although some attention would be paid to soil problems in the latter. The emphasis was to fall on practical demonstration and development, rather than on additional investigation. The plan received treasury approval and early in July was officially submitted to the Dar es Salaam representative of the Special Fund. It outlined a scheme in which the government and Special Fund would roughly match one another's contributions, totaling some $2 million spread over three years. After adding a section, advised by the representative of the WHO in Dar es Salaam, to cover epidemiological factors, especially bilharzia, and after weathering some further "acting up" by the "backroom" of the Special Fund,[4] the plan was approved by the Managing Director for submission to the Governing Council in January 1964. By this time, the Special Fund component had grown slightly and the FAO was designated as the operating agency. On 25 January 1964, the approval of the project by the Governing Council was communicated to the government, and in mid-April the plan of operations was signed. The project could then go ahead.

Despite the heavy investment of time and effort during the three years required to develop the Wami-Pangani survey, it did not stand out after its completion as a highly successful magnet for investment. Interviews conducted in 1966 and 1967 in Dar es Salaam indicated that international officials with an overview of UNDP activities were sceptical of its outcome. The survey and irrigation pilot scheme apparently did not proceed smoothly to a successful or useful conclusion. One official of the project, it was said, simply severed his area of responsibility from the rest and followed his own ideas, formed during earlier years of experience in Tanganyika. A great deal of pressure was put on him to conform to the standards as interpreted by the Project Manager and the UNDP office, but without much success. The project, originally designed for three years, ended at the close of 1967.

[4] Quotations from an internal communication emanating from an international official in the agricultural ministry.

The Tanzanian Five Year Plan, published in 1969, shows a markedly different accent from its predecessor.[5] It reflects the approach of the Arusha Declaration, emphasizing "African socialism" and cooperative approaches which the government believed would fit best with the tribal and peasant background of the Tanzanians. It is almost innocent of any reference to the outcome of the 555 man-months of expert services put into the survey. No outside investment had been attracted to the two valleys. Some irrigated land, an outcome of the pilot projects, was in use, and the government planned to extend the irrigation schemes. Nevertheless, given the approach of the Arusha Declaration and the lack of enthusiasm about the outcome of the survey, it seems unlikely that development of the valleys will be able to attract large-scale financing.

Two lines of explanation, one of them relating primarily to international administration and the other to Tanzanian jurisdiction, appear to bear on the modest outcome of this large-scale project. The project was never deftly handled in the international administration. It caused friction between the field representative and the FAO hierarchy and among its divisions. The Resident Representative was hard put to find compromises, but, in part because each proposal tended to be watered down by competing ideas, the final plan lacked coherence. Furthermore, the FAO had trouble administering it as a unit, and one field officer charged with management proved unamenable to instructions. None

[5] *Tanzania Second Five-Year Plan for Economic and Social Development 1st July, 1969–30th June, 1974*, 2 vols. (Dar es Salaam: Government Printer, 1969). The speech by Nyerere to the TANU (party) conference, pp. vii–xxiii, makes clear the differences between the new orientation and the previous plan.

110

of this was unknown to the Tanzanian government and probably decreased the prestige of the venture.

At the same time, the Tanzanian government revised its approach to development in such a way as to diminish the importance of the ideas underlying the Wami-Pangani survey. As originally conceived, the plan in the end would have required large-scale financing to spread the effects of demonstration farms and to make the most of water sources. Such sums simply were not available in the Tanzanian economy and would have had to have been imported, along with new technology. Development of agriculture from a cooperative, peasant base was not the central idea of the Wami-Pangani survey. The survey therefore did not fit well with the new ideas of the government and became a casualty of change. This shows that the approach favored by the FAO had not become an integral part of Tanzanian thinking and suggests a low level of permanent influence.

SHAPING PROJECT DIMENSIONS: MALAWI

The case of the Lower Shire Valley in Malawi includes many of the same elements that were present in the Wami-Pangani survey in Tanzania, but the ending was quite different. In Malawi, the IDA eventually made low interest loans. Here the preinvestment strategy worked, at least to the point of obtaining credits for a project developed in the UNDP context. Yet the development of the project proceeded in anything but a smooth manner. Unlike the surveys in Tanzania and Zambia, it involved the head of the government, Prime Minister H. Kamazu Banda (now President Banda), almost from the beginning and it provoked considerable conflict among the international agencies. During this conflict the dimensions of the project underwent several revisions, some of them demanded by the Malawi government and others by one or the other of the international organizations.

Because the Shire Valley project, like the Luangwa and Wami-Pangani surveys, involved agricultural and water development, the FAO was a key organization. In contrast to the role it played in the Tanzanian and Zambian projects, however, the World Bank exerted a direct influence on the plans. In the Luangwa and Wami-Pangani instances, influence from the IBRD remained indirect, as far as can be learned, confined to the routine practice of sending the draft plan of operations to the World Bank for comment. Nothing in the available record shows that such comments had any important effect. Furthermore, while expatriate civil servants of the Tanzanian and Zambian governments had a leading role, they had less decisive influence than in Malawi. There the remaining contingent of British colonial servants expected to stay on for a considerable time and knew that the narrow educational and training pipeline could only slowly turn out their replacements. Moreover, most of the ministers in the government had little confidence in their own ability to make decisions and constantly referred issues to the Prime Minister, who lacked neither confidence nor power. Finally, the small scale of the country, its isolation, its lack of economic promise, and the Prime Minister's policy of treating relations with South Africa and Rhodesia in a particularly gentle manner did not necessarily inspire the international agencies to put their best foot forward. Nevertheless, a Resident Representative was stationed in Zomba and was expected to show some results.

The Lower Shire Valley project appears to have originated in August 1964, when K.D.S. Baldwin, economic adviser to the government under United Nations auspices, visited FAO headquarters in Rome, where he was well known as a former official and consultant. The FAO suggested that three men be sent as a technical assistance team to work up a survey of the Lower Shire Valley and the Elephant Marsh area, a flat, swampy section lying south of Blantyre on the river's slowly winding route to the Zambezi. A survey of the area was not a novel idea, but when the FAO followed an official request of the government with efforts to put together a team that would emphasize agriculture, the Prime Minister objected. He wanted a request for a loan to the World Bank. When the bureaucratic procedure was explained by the head of the FAO mission, who arrived in November, and others, the process of putting together a request for a Special Fund project went ahead.

Despite some misgivings from FAO headquarters, the Prime Minister in January 1965 officially requested a Special Fund preinvestment project for the valley. A personal letter went from Banda to David Owen, long-time head of the UNTAB and later Associate Administrator of the UNDP. Kouros Satrap, the Resident Representative at that time, supported the project and hoped that it might be approved at the June 1965 meeting of the Governing Council. But the FAO's misgivings became more serious, and Rome requested the government to spell out the economic and social benefits expected from the project. This view was shared by the Special Fund in New York. It led to a show of displeasure on the part of the Prime Minister, who refused to accede to that request. Eventually, in March, two Malawi ministers, the Ambassador to the United Nations and a financial

113

adviser from Zomba met officials of the Special Fund in New York. The ministers were told that the request could not go before the June meeting of the Governing Council without revision but that the Special Fund would support a new four-month FAO mission to produce a different, more technical basis for the request. The team arrived early in August and three weeks later had drafted a request which included a variety of pilot projects and a shift of emphasis to dry agriculture.

This draft produced a three-way split among the FAO sponsored experts, the government, and a representative from Rome of the joint World Bank-FAO division. The survey team thought that the scope of the project should be broader. The World Bank representative promptly pointed out that now the tendency was to go much farther than just reclamation, which was all that could be financed. The Prime Minister, who was presented with the eventual draft for signature, disliked pilot projects and lengthy surveys, which he associated with the FAO. He therefore extracted from the international officials a commitment to produce some concrete proposals. Eventually, on 23 August 1965, a new request was signed by Banda. This project for a survey and pilot work on irrigation and agriculture was approved in January 1966 in New York, and recruitment of personnel began while the plan of operations was being drafted.

This stage produced sharp conflict between the government and the FAO and led to decisive intervention by the World Bank. In February 1966, Malawi officials informed the Resident Representative that the Minister of Natural Resources saw the project in new terms. Immediate action and results were wanted, not questionable pilot projects. Soon afterward the Malawi government aid coordinator objected to the delays in recruiting personnel to get started on the project. This move appeared to be an attempt to hurry the Special Fund into action, but the UNDP clearly was embarrassed about the lack of a plan of operations on which to proceed. The task of drafting such a plan had been given to the FAO, which meanwhile had decided to send a group from its IBRD/FAO division to examine the project. By mid-April this group had drafted a plan of operations.

At this point, the Prime Minister again intervened. Banda insisted on a concentration on irrigation in the Lower Shire Valley and on the exclusion of experimental studies. Moreover, he wanted the IBRD, which then had a Development Advisory Service (DAS) team in Malawi to examine another project,[6] to study the Lower Shire proposals. The government's position now was based on the association of the IBRD, and in particular the DAS, with the Lower Shire. In May, the government, which in this instance means that the Prime Minister had been consulted, cabled the FAO, asking for a radical revision of the entire project and for a discussion in New York. This meeting took place in early June in Rome.

It soon became clear that the Malawi government was trying to prevent the FAO from taking over the survey as the executing agency. It would accept joint FAO–IBRD participation in planning the survey and also wanted the Lower Shire project linked with the

---

[6] The DAS was established in Nairobi by the IBRD to provide consultant service to member governments. Its personnel for the most part consisted of experienced officials who had earlier worked for the colonial governments. It thus retained the skills of colonial officials while denaturing their political status.

Lilongwe development scheme in which the DAS was busy.[7]

A crisis was reached in mid-July. An FAO representative told the officials of the Ministry of Natural Resources in Malawi that the decision as to which division of the FAO would deal with the problem was an internal matter not for discussion. After more consideration, the FAO agreed with the Ministry on a compromise. An outside consulting firm should be engaged by the FAO and the UNDP to carry out the survey.[8] The argument dragged on until September, when at last a plan of operation was drafted and signed. Responsibility for the survey was to be given to a consulting firm, but the question of which firm to choose led to further differences. Eventually, Lockwood Survey Corporation of Canada undertook the work, which was finished in 1969.

The actual survey of the irrigation district was linked, as the government with the growing support of the World Bank wished, with a 3,500-acre rain-watered cotton area in the Lower Shire Valley and with the survey of 500,000 acres in Lilongwe. The motivating force for the combination of the three projects and for reduction

[7] The Lilongwe project was an agricultural development scheme, not coincidentally sited in the province where the new capital of Malawi would be placed.

[8] Under UNDP regulations, it is possible to employ private firms to carry out contracts. The specialized agencies in effect compete with private contractors in seeking responsibility for Special Fund projects. Although it was unusual for a private contractor to be given this sort of work in East and Central Africa, the formula provided a way for the FAO to keep its association with the Shire Valley survey and yet give assurance to Banda that it would not be altogether in charge of either the field work or the eventual report.

of the FAO's share in performing the survey work came from the World Bank, whose officials were increasingly in evidence in Rome and in Zomba after the crisis of mid-July 1966. The Bank's Development Advisory Service had carried out the Lilongwe survey, which was completed in 1966, along with the work in the cotton area of the Lower Shire. The entire project cost some $2.6 million, of which the UNDP contributed $1.8 million.

In the Malawi surveys case, the principles of the UNDP preinvestment strategy clearly had determining value. Both the Lilongwe scheme and the cotton area scheme were funded by loans from the IDA in 1968. For the latter scheme, a loan of $3.7 million was made, based on repayment over forty years with a ten-year grace period. The Lilongwe scheme was given $6 million on similar terms. The IDA agreed to consider and then granted a loan for the Lower Shire irrigation scheme for the 1970–1971 financial year.

Yet the procedures differed substantially from the formal model. The IBRD was heavily involved at a very early stage in the survey, not near its end or at its conclusion. This involvement did not result primarily from favorable survey results or inviting prospects but rather because Banda regarded the FAO's methods as slow and impractical. The FAO's response apparently was calculated to demonstrate that its expertise should be the guide and that Malawi could accept it or not much else. This opened the way for IBRD representatives to exert heavy influence on the project. The thin theoretical content of the approach used by the Malawi government formally had little in common with the policies of the FAO or the IBRD. Its very thinness provided

117

room for maneuver, rather than a clear indication of which organization logically should prevail. Nevertheless, the outcome may prove highly beneficial to Malawi and, in the short term, obviously gave a good return in IBRD financing.

4.

INFLUENCE: ADVICE AND CRISIS

With the exception of loans from the World Bank system, the primary means by which all international organization projects aid governments with economic development is advice and compilation and analysis of specialized information. It is therefore an effort to introduce new technology or to make more efficient the existing methods of economic production and social administration. The advice proffered generally has to do with problems that have been defined by means of interactions among governments and international organizations over a considerable period of time. This process, discussed in Chapter 3, is presumed to be a means of keeping the character of advice specific to a defined problem, rather than opening the way to across-the-board recommendations from international personnel. The aims of a particular project may be wide in terms of local social effects, as with the river valley projects, which were intended to open new farming plots, increase agricultural production, protect natural resources, and train personnel. Yet each component was precisely defined and the boundaries of the project carefully marked out.

Despite the specificity demanded by a project approach, international organizations have furnished advisers and advice that have to do with the functioning of the whole economy. This is the effect of advisory services often furnished by the IMF, for example. In

119

the three observed countries, advisers with wide mandates were furnished to the governments, and the Resident Representatives also sometimes offered such advice. This chapter will illustrate such broad scale advisory work, which in a sense runs counter to the principle of closely defined technical assistance built around economic planning for recipient countries. In addition, the chapter will give attention to assistance to Zambia in relation to the effects of the political crisis caused by the Unilateral Declaration of Independence in Rhodesia in 1965.

ADVISING ON GENERAL DEVELOPMENTAL PROBLEMS

An economic adviser to the government was at work in each of the three countries investigated during all or part of the observation period. In Malawi and Zambia, this official was appointed under the OPEX scheme and thus served as a national civil servant subsidized by the international organization. (In Tanzania, he was furnished under a bilateral scheme.) Formally, he had no relationship to the Resident Representative or any international organization insofar as his work or responsibility were concerned. Unlike technical assistance advisers, of whom there were as many as forty at work at any time, OPEX officials made no periodic or final reports to any agency in the UN system and were not provided with counterparts to be trained. Like technical assistance advisers but unlike Special Fund project personnel, they had short-term assignments, usually a year at a time, which might, however, be renewed.

Despite their special status (closely resembling that of a former official of a colonial service who was kept on under contract status by a newly independent government), the OPEX advisers did have some connection with the Resident Representatives. This begins with inclusion of the latter's advice in the original request for the post, and that advice would also bear on any renewal. Furthermore, OPEX officials tended to keep up close relations with the community of international and expatriate officials with whom they had professional and cultural ties. OPEX personnel usually were regarded by the expatriates sent or lent by national governments as not quite part of their own ranks but more allied with the international officials whose status, the expatriates often pretended, was vague and privileged. Finally, no foreign official—expatriate, international civil servant, or OPEX—can enter completely into the political and cultural practices of his host African country, if for no other reason than his lack of an indispensable role during the crucial agitation and organization for independence.

In Malawi during 1964–1966, the general economic adviser, K.D.S. Baldwin, had the title of Economic Adviser to the Prime Minister (later President). A former British civil servant with experience in Nigeria, Baldwin's connections with the FAO came into play in writing the plan of operations for the Lower Shire Valley project. His appointment in Malawi resulted from his acquaintance with Kamazu Banda during an FAO mission to the country. Baldwin's title was intended to suggest a close relationship with the head of the government, rather than that of a specialist. Other national and international civil servants confirmed that Baldwin regarded his functions as depending on loyalty and service to Banda, rather than to the cabinet or the whole government.

Baldwin believed that his appointment through the

121

international organization system gave him valuable protection from the pressure that grew out of the presence of the expatriate British civil servants in Malawi.[1] If he had been associated with that group, his freedom to advise the Prime Minister would have been limited. His advice sometimes ran counter to the general feeling in the expatriate group, especially on matters requiring economic analysis and quantitative estimates. Baldwin was the only economist near the top of the government, and he found some difficulty both in persuading civil servants with differing backgrounds and in making projections without adequate statistics. Moreover, the expatriate civil servants had always to think of their relations with the British High Commission, then the source of a large annual subsidy for Malawi government operations. If Baldwin indicated a certain distrust of the expatriate group, some of them thought of him as a "hatchet man" for the Prime Minister and as inappropriately deep in political affairs.

Because Baldwin defended the range and flexibility of his advisory mandate, depending on the Prime Minister's needs, his work could not be done without producing some opposition. That he had enemies in the civil service, which was effectively British at that time, could hardly be overlooked. Some of his critics thought

---

[1] No claim that any single opinion prevailed among the expatriate British civil servants is made. They could, however, be distinguished from other advisers and civil servants in that they were civil servants of the United Kingdom government, for the most part from the former Colonial Service; they were the last generation of such colonial civil servants; they were primarily administrative officers, rather than substantive specialists, e.g., economists, although some were in fact specialists; and, at least because of their numbers, they were conspicuous.

he "pulled strings" to make the government and the civil service act according to his ideas.

Despite the strength with which such views were sometimes expressed, it was difficult to uncover much more than vague information about precisely what political activity was in question. No informant suggested, for example, that Banda's unheated reaction to South African influence in Malawi and the maintenance of several kinds of economic ties with South Africa, Mozambique, and Rhodesia had economic effects which the Prime Minister's adviser might have analyzed. Rather, domestic politics and, more often, appointments of personnel seemed to give rise to comments about Baldwin's special position.

In the narrow world of international development specialists and largely expatriate senior civil servants in Malawi, it was inevitable that personal characteristics and differences should take on importance. The actions of each individual visibly affected those of others. Each official knew every other at least to some degree and often very well, and the flow of communication within this group was remarkably quick. The replacement of any official had necessarily to bring about discernible changes in the practices of his office.

As a consequence, Baldwin's relations with the Resident Representative depended to a considerable extent on the degree to which the two officials found their ideas and practices compatible. The amount of information that Baldwin would furnish the Resident Representative was related to his degree of personal trust in the international official and his belief that the latter could be of help. It was obvious that Baldwin was closer to Gordon Menzies, who arrived in 1966, than to his predecessor, Kouros Satrap. Baldwin had a broad knowledge of the operations of the Malawi government and detailed information on the ideas of the Prime Minister. If he used this inside knowledge indiscretely, it would soon become known and his usefulness in Malawi would end abruptly. If, on the other hand, he failed to use it to help the Resident Representative do his work better, Baldwin would sacrifice a possible advantage in getting development aid for Malawi. He did keep Satrap informed to some extent of his activities, but deliberately avoided, to the chagrin of the Resident Representative, any kind of regular reporting or systematic consultation. Satrap believed that his own relations with the Prime Minister were both close and influential. Baldwin was less than enthusiastic about this appreciation on the part of the Resident Representative and had no intention of relaying his conversations with the Prime Minister. As a consequence, each man regarded the other with some wariness.

The relationship between Menzies and Baldwin became obviously closer and more confident as the two men worked together. Baldwin remarked that cooperating with the UN office provided better results, because Menzies, who had headed the technical assistance recruitment office in Geneva, had been more effective in finding good quality advisers. Menzies received from Baldwin a general idea of the slant of economic negotiations in progress without the details that would trouble the confidential relationship between the adviser and the Prime Minister. By late 1966, both Baldwin and Menzies, as well as others in a position to know, were reaching the conclusion that Baldwin's usefulness was coming to an end. They believed that after two years the influence and effectiveness of an independent economic

124

adviser begins to decline. By the end of 1966, Baldwin had become head of the Malawi Development Corporation, leaving behind much of his direct influence on a broad spectrum of economic policy.

During his service as economic adviser, Baldwin had become concerned with several important developments. These included the formation of the Malawi Development Corporation, the creation of a better statistical service, the IDA loans for the Lilongwe and Shire Valley projects, and the negotiation of the South African share in financing the development of a new national capital at Lilongwe. He had direct responsibility for none of these projects. Yet he obviously had been consulted and probably was a primary influence, if for no other reason than the paucity of competent analysts. With the exception of the new capital at Lilongwe, all of these projects fitted with programs of the UN system. As for South African or Rhodesian influence, he showed little enthusiasm for the attempts of political organs of the United Nations to give a special shape to national politics. He had worked closely with the Resident Representative on some matters but in no sense had assumed a subordinate role or had received instructions. The constraints on him were far more professional and political than those of international discipline or organizational doctrine.

Meanwhile, in Zambia, a Canadian professor of economics, Gordon Goundry, served as economic adviser to the government. Some of his experiences and problems resembled those of Baldwin, while others reflected special local situations. Goundry took up his assignment in 1964, after it was certain that the Central African Federation, with which he did not want to be associated, would disappear, and stayed on for two years

125

through the excitement of independence. As a consequence, Goundry, like Baldwin, knew both the new African politicians and officials and the remaining expatriate civil servants. In other respects, the atmosphere in which the two advisers worked differed sharply, especially with regard to rapid Africanization, which the Zambian government favored, and to relations with Rhodesia and South Africa. The expectation that the all-white government of Rhodesia would eventually declare independence and cause a general political crisis in central Africa inevitably colored thoughts about economic and social development during Goundry's tenure.

Goundry viewed his task as having an educational purpose, for he often spoke of the need to introduce top figures of the government and the civil service to analytical approaches to economic problems. At one stage, he directed a series of meetings, which had the function of seminars, for ministers and top officials. He acted as a general adviser and did not, as Baldwin had done, try to make the point that he was an adviser to the President, rather than the government. Nevertheless, like Baldwin, he became a controversial figure and willingly accepted the notion that his usefulness in the job was probably limited to two years.

Despite his own attempt to define his job broadly, Goundry became increasingly identified with President Kenneth Kaunda. In part, that was the outcome to be expected in a government headed by a man as talented and attractive as Kaunda. It was also a result of the shortage of skilled manpower that was so much a feature of African governments in the 1960s; a skillful analyst with broad knowledge was immediately adopted by one or the other of the stronger leaders. Goundry found that the former colonial servants on the whole

had so little experience in dealing with political questions that he frequently was forced to consult the President rather than a leading ministry official about the
acceptability of a policy that he had in mind. Goundry's
growing association with the main sources of decisions
in the cabinet, and especially in the person of Kaunda,
brought him into a number of overtly political situations. Even though he was sent by the United Nations
and was an expatriate, he was asked to attend as an
adviser the Victoria Falls Conference of 1964, which
prepared the separation of Zambia from Rhodesia.

From that time on, Goundry often traveled with the
President, even on trips abroad, and prepared drafts of
speeches for him. He served in other ways as a presidential aide and also was asked at one stage to negotiate
with Tanzanian authorities with regard to the highly
political plans for the TanZam Railroad, connecting
Zambia with the port at Dar es Salaam. Goundry also
thought it part of his duty as adviser to urge contingency planning in the event of Rhodesian independence
but believed that little was done in the way of preparing
transport and stockpiles of materials.

In order to protect his freedom to give advice,
Goundry adopted the tactic of never relaying his conversations with ministers, to whom he generally had
easy access, to permanent secretaries and vice versa. In
this way, he would not directly contradict the advice
of civil servants and bring about confrontations which
would be generally embarrassing. Yet this tactic led to
situations in which permanent secretaries could not
understand how ministers were making decisions, and
Goundry eventually was suspected of manipulating the
cabinet. Furthermore, two ministers found themselves
unable to get approval for certain favorite plans because

127

of his advice and tended thereafter to oppose him. Goundry concluded, therefore, that over time his usefulness would decline, perhaps very sharply, and he was prepared, as adviser, to be sacrificed if someone had to bear the blame for a wrong decision.

Goundry's outlook on economic planning for development in the LDCs also indirectly tended to arouse criticism. He strongly opposed reliance on sophisticated quantitative methods in planning because of the absence, noted also by Baldwin, of good statistics. Moreover, he believed that much planning overlooked the inelasticity of supply, typical in LDCs. The right approach would be to make indicative plans for the long term, never expecting the same degree of accuracy in forecasting that was achieved in highly developed countries. For the short term, development plans should be identical to the government budget, in which the finance ministry must inevitably have the last word. The various ministries must have the primary responsibility for developing projects, and the planning office should coordinate them. The economic adviser should confine himself to working out the economic consequences of development goals, which are political matters, and not try to impose them.

This approach left Goundry open to criticism from several directions. Although he considered most of the Zambian civil servants and ministers with whom he worked insufficiently skilled in economic analysis and quantitative methods, he nevertheless opposed a small group of econometrically-trained expatriate economists who wanted to use sophisticated methods. By emphasizing the importance of economic analysis of development plans, however, he disturbed the old line civil servants whose generalist outlook tended to emphasize

128

the maintenance of law and order and good management techniques within the ministries. Because of his closeness to the President and his policy of discretion about selecting goals, he left little documentary evidence of his work. One high planning official and a civil servant who operated at cabinet level each remarked that Goundry had had little influence because he had not left behind papers which guided governmental policies. At the same time, a senior British consultant who had been trained in the Indian civil service noted that Goundry and his like lacked the practical experience needed to do a good job in developing an economy. The emphasis on systematic analysis, he said, was too theoretical to do any good.

Goundry himself was aware of the kind of criticism his efforts were arousing, as was the Resident Representative, with whom he was in close touch. He often traded thoughts with UN personnel and passed along some information of use in conducting projects in the international organization orbit. The relationship that grew up appeared to be one of trust and mutual respect, but certainly not one of comment, proposal, and response. The decision that he should not be appointed for another two years was discussed with the Resident Representative and made on the basis of mutual agreement.

RESIDENT REPRESENTATIVE AS ADVISER

Although George Ivan Smith, and to a lesser degree, Kouros Satrap, tended to emphasize the representational aspects of their assignments, the main preoccupation of the Resident Representatives was with the day-to-day management of the programs under their jurisdiction.[2] Their formal assignment during the period under observation was to help governments formulate requests for assistance in a form that could be accepted by the UNDP and to serve as the senior UN official in their areas. Their international status gave them, on the one hand, an independence that the economic advisers to the governments, working within the national government structures, did not have. On the other hand, international status limited their ability to serve the local government, and, as has been seen in the Wami-Pangani survey, they sometimes found themselves squeezed between governments and international organizations. This dual status called for a certain creativity and artfulness in finding ways out of impasses and offered some opportunity for deliberately trying to influence the host government. The politicians and officials of the host governments soon came to understand that if they allowed themselves to be persuaded by a Resident Representative, they might also press their own programs more effectively. From this mutual understanding emerged the faint outlines of a unique political symbiosis.

If the influence of economic advisers derived primarily from their ability to use analytical techniques in ways that had political relevance for government leaders, the Resident Representatives lacked an analogous advantage. They rarely had the skills or the background on which to base a technical economic analysis. Usually, their skills and experience related to the operations of international organizations and the techniques and manners of their bureaucracies. Their formal assignments from the UNDP—to help governments formulate

2 See Chapter 2, pp. 67–75.

130

suitable requests for aid—emphasized these bureaucratic skills. Furthermore, none of the Resident Representatives had an intimate knowledge of the operations of the IBRD, although they usually were familiar with the situations in other agencies. As a consequence, the Residence Representatives were most useful to governments when a difficulty arose in proposing, formulating, or altering a UNDP project. They were only infrequently consulted on the economic development program as a whole and never, so far as available material indicated, in a planned and formal way.[3] Nevertheless, the Resident Representatives and their staffs invariably paid strict attention to the economic plans adopted by the host governments and often were informed, sometimes by international personnel, of the ideas and approaches that were being considered for incorporation in the plans. There are some indications that consultations with the planners may have helped to incorporate proposals that were potentially suitable for aid from international organizations.

The Resident Representatives tried hard to keep abreast of political developments in their territories and reported routinely on them every quarter or half year to the UNDP. From time to time, if there were heightened political tensions, e.g., the revolt in Zanzibar or the Rhodesian declaration of independence, special reports were sent to the United Nations Headquarters. With his political brief, Ivan Smith gave far more at-

---

[3] The Jackson Report, Vol. 1, pp. 20-21, 26, proposes strong steps to make the Resident Representative the focal point of national economic planning as it relates to international assistance. In effect, the position described here would be reversed. The UNDP Governing Council showed obvious reluctance to adopting such a proposal in its strongest form.

tention to such reporting than his successors did. His communications usually were addressed to the Secretary-General. Whether such communications had any impact on the development of policy by the Secretary-General is difficult to say. The Secretary-General had no significant resources for analyzing such field intelligence, and only very rarely was any comment received by a Resident Representative.[4] With the exception of Ivan Smith, most Resident Representatives went out of their way to avoid an overtly political role. One or two went so far as to discourage any attempts on the part of governments to treat them as representatives of the United Nations as a whole. The arrival of political officials from United Nations Headquarters or the scheduling of a meeting by such bodies as the Committee of 24 on Colonialism was regarded by the field staffs as an unnecessary "circus" on which they would unavoidably have to waste some time.

Yet a curious duality in views could frequently be detected. Every Resident Representative in Lusaka (as well as the rest of the staffs posted there), for example, expressed the view that the region had particular political importance because of the Rhodesian situation and the influence of South Africa. That Botswana, Lesotho, and Swaziland formally were part of the district supervised from Lusaka only heightened this impression. "We are a window on the south," one Resident Representative remarked. For the whole period under observation, the window was so wide open that it was possible to telephone Salisbury and South Africa without difficulty, and from time to time this communication link was used

[4] See comments in Leon Gordenker, *The UN Secretary-General and the Maintenance of Peace* (New York: Columbia University Press, 1967), 152–56.

to deal with leftover problems from the Rhodesian program or an unusual emergency. South African officials
in Malawi, however, sought no contact with the UN
staff or advisers; these were regarded with some reason
as representing an enemy of the South African regime.
In Dar es Salaam, the presence of revolutionary liberation movements also opened a window to the south.
Although little direct contact between these groups and
international organization personnel was observed, information about the activities of liberation movements
could hardly be avoided in the network of diplomatic
contacts. While this background presence was felt constantly by the Resident Representatives, none of them
was under any illusion that assistance to the governments that opposed Rhodesia and South Africa would
have any decisive effect on international relations in
southern Africa. "We do what we can," said one official
in Lusaka, where the office was charged with assisting
the official UN relief program for refugees from South
Africa. The atmosphere never became that of a crusade
but rather one of a search for a marginal benefit here
and there in the opposition to South Africa. Nor was
there any overt desire on the part of most international
personnel to go much beyond those limits.

A sharp political crisis or an unexpected event which
attracts attention abroad can promptly increase the
political role of Resident Representatives. For two or
three days after the 1964 coup d'état in Zanzibar, which
ultimately led to union with Tanganyika, one of the few
sources of information available to the rest of the world
was the handful of advisers furnished by the UN system
to the island. It became possible for the office in Dar
es Salaam to send officials to Zanzibar in relation to the
program there. The by-product of these visits was a

glance at events, reported to New York, in a territory that was otherwise almost inaccessible. Similarly, in Rhodesia during the months before UDI, and even afterwards, it was possible for a few UN officials to remain in contact with developments in Salisbury. Whether such activities on the part of personnel sent to the three countries for development purposes had any unusual impact on the policies adopted by the Secretary-General or other UN organs is doubtful. However, the pace of information-seeking and the level of interest markedly increased in the field offices.

Because the Resident Representatives had special competence in dealing with the decision process in international organizations, it might be thought that they would develop additional influence by helping governments prepare their policies and brief their delegations for meetings at the distant headquarters. Ivan Smith was able to discuss forthcoming General Assembly and Security Council meetings with government leaders on some occasions. Evidence that other Resident Representatives from time to time discussed problems and agendas with national delegations also appeared. But such discussion and briefings were exceptional and only sporadic, depending mainly on fortuitous circumstances. Moreover, it was not apparent that the Resident Representatives or their staffs possessed any special information or even a thorough working knowledge of the vast international organization documentation. They could obtain what was necessary from headquarters and did receive certain documentation relating to development problems as a matter of course. But of the three observed, only the Dar es Salaam office had a useful collection of documents, and that was only because of the existence of a United Nations Information

Center which had been established independent of the UNDP. On the government side, there was equally little evidence of careful following and use of documentation and reports from international organizations. In important matters of policy, such as events in Rhodesia, the national officials charged with preparing decisions had communications from national missions in New York. For less sharply defined matters, such as resolutions of the Economic and Social Council, information was much more difficult to obtain.

Furthermore, it was exceptional to see copies of specialized agency reports or those of the International Bank in the hands of national officials. These were transmitted to the governments in a routine way, but busy civil servants had little time to give to them, even if the distribution systems worked well. This is not to say that technical reports had no influence at all but rather to underline the sporadic and unsystematic use of such material.

Meeting a Crisis: UDI in Rhodesia

The Unilateral Declaration of Independence in November 1965, by what the United Nations has since characterized as the illegal authorities in Salisbury, had been long anticipated in the UNDP office in Lusaka. However carefully staged and bolstered with the rhetoric of the settlers in Rhodesia, it was an event with obvious political overtones for southern Africa. The General Assembly had long been busy with resolutions to encourage or pressure the United Kingdom to act against the rebels in its colony.[5] Yet none of the reso-

[5] See United Nations General Assembly Resolutions 2012 (XX) (1965); 2002 (XX); and resolutions cited in the latter.

135

lutions adopted by the General Assembly or the Security Council before or after the event referred directly to the several economic development programs from which Rhodesia received aid.

These programs were primarily products of the days of the Central African Federation and had aims related to the whole territory, although advisers and facilities were located in Rhodesia or on its borders. The most important project was the Kariba Fisheries Institute, which sought to develop the products of the lake created by the Kariba Dam. The dam itself had been built with the support of a loan from the IBRD. In addition, a handful of advisers dealt with a series of agricultural projects, and in the University of Rhodesia and Nyasaland, UNESCO provided strong financial and moral backing for a nonracial Institute of Education. Altogether, this set of projects made no great splash in the pool of development aid available to Africa as a whole, but on the local scale it was substantial enough to be visible.

Immediately after UDI, the Security Council acted on a British initiative, representing a sharp twist in previous policy, to condemn the Ian Smith regime and to urge all states to refrain from aiding it. Eventually, the Security Council decided that UDI represented a threat to peace and imposed economic sanctions on Rhodesia. No specific instructions were issued to the UNDP, the Specialized Agencies, or the IBRD complex.[6]

[6] See short account in *Yearbook of the United Nations 1965* (New York: United Nations, 1966), 124–28; and UN Security Council Resolutions 202 (1965), 216 (1965), and 217 (1965). UN Security Council Resolution 232 (1966) called on Specialized Agencies to report measures supporting limited sanctions

Nevertheless, the Resident Representative's office in Lusaka at once issued orders to all personnel in Rhodesia to withdraw. The New York headquarters was informed of this action, which had been prepared in advance. Richard Symonds, then in charge at Lusaka, went personally to Salisbury to discuss with officials of the external affairs department the breaking off of UN programs. He met a chilly and tense group in Salisbury, but there was no doubt about the position of either side and no attempt to interfere with the withdrawal of personnel. All technical advisers appeared in Lusaka within a short time, as did the personnel of the Institute of Education at Salisbury. The latter became a part of the fledgling University of Zambia, and its director, Professor Cyril Rogers, soon won the confidence and trust of President Kaunda, who sometimes sought his advice on broad political questions as well as those related to the work of the Institute and the University. Other technical advisers, fewer than ten, received new assignments in Zambia. In effect, the assistance given Zambia had been increased markedly.

The Fisheries Institute proved to be a more complicated affair. It was located on the man-made lake contained by the Kariba Dam, and its opposite shores were controlled by Rhodesia and Zambia. Although the Institute's main buildings were on the north, Zambian,

---

against Rhodesia, and Resolution 253 (1968), ordering general sanctions, asked the agencies to aid Zambia. The Report of the Secretary-General on the implementation of Resolution 232 (UN Document S/7781 and addenda and corrections, 21 Feb. 1967) noted that Zambia had special problems arising from UDI and reported that UNDP had sent special consultants to help. Malawi also reported having to carry on some trade with Rhodesia.

bank of the lake, some of its work took place in Rhodesian installations. In any case, free access to the lake waters, regardless of ownership, was necessary for full investigation and study. The director of the institute at first accepted the political aims of cutting Rhodesia out of the benefits of the Institute's work and accommodated himself to the directives received from the Resident Representative. Within a short time, however, the work of this UNDP-supported Institute became restricted because of the hostile atmosphere at Lake Kariba and some of its staff began advising the Zambian government on other projects. Later the director let it be known that the politically motivated change in assignment had nullified the expected work of the Institute, and he expressed open doubt about the wisdom and value of the move.

The Zambian government clearly had new needs, which were quickly assessed in Lusaka. In these circumstances, the UNDP office followed Ivan Smith's practice of offering maximum support to the local government. Such support clearly was in line with the general policies of the United Nations and accorded with the advice that Ivan Smith had given to New York. The result was that the UNDP technical assistance program in Zambia expanded rapidly. By the end of 1966 the increase in technical assistance expenditures, as compared with the previous year, amounted to 130 per cent, including the personnel made available from Rhodesia. A number of short-term advisory missions, initiated by the UN Economic Commission for Africa and by the IBRD, also were mounted.

In several instances, the technical advisers who were recruited immediately after UDI had tasks directly related to the emergency. Although such advisers had not been sought to plan a response to UDI, they now were consulted in connection with transportation, power, and mining operations. The most important rail connection between Zambia and coast, as well as with South Africa, ran through Rhodesian territory. The secondary connection to the west coast crossed Portuguese territory. Both the Rhodesian and Portuguese authorities might be expected, under certain circumstances, to interfere with the rail operations, cutting off vital imports and blocking the flow of copper, Zambia's source of foreign exchange. Moreover, the possibility that the Rhodesian authorities might switch off power from the Kariba Dam intensified the search for alternative sources. Similarly, Zambian mines used Rhodesian coal; at least a partial substitute was sought and developed in Zambia.

A clear example of an adviser connected with the emergency was Professor John Mars, who was brought from the Economic Commission for Africa as economic adviser to the government. Much of his work was concerned with the problem of transportation. He helped to develop an alternate truck-rail route to the east to connect with the rail head in Malawi, using the Great East Road, for which an improvement loan from the IDA was made available. From there, the port of Beira in Mozambique could be reached. He took part in some of the negotiations between the two estranged governments. Mars also gave advice on the northbound road, the "Hell Route" of some journalistic fame, that went along the Great North Road through Mpika to Dar es Salaam. Both of these roadways proved of some use in getting copper out and supplies in, although the costs

139

remained very high. An ebullient figure, Mars took it as his mandate to explore unusual and obscure remedies for Zambian difficulties. He appeared to have some success in uncovering new possibilities and in persuading the government of their potential.

The emergency did not, however, substantially affect the doubts with which the IBRD had been viewing proposals for a rail connection through Tanzania to the coast. Goundry had offered some advice on this plan earlier, and Mars knew of the negotiations, which increasingly involved the People's Republic of China, from where the necessary financing was eventually obtained. The Resident Representatives during the period from 1965 to 1967 made it a point to keep informed on the negotiations and in general favored the Zambian-Tanzanian claims that such a railroad would have the greatest importance in economic development as well as in reducing Zambian dependence on Rhodesia and South Africa.

With respect to Zambia's needs and fears, the services of the Resident Representatives and the other parts of the UN system, including the IBRD, were unimpressive. This was made obvious by Zambian estimates that the sanctions imposed by the Security Council were costing the country more than £27 million per year.[7] Fuel subsidies alone, to make up for the difficulty in transport, were costing £14 million per year.[8] The economic plan, based on copper sales and free access to the usual transportation methods, turned into little more than waste paper. That difficulties of this character would result from a strong stand against UDI was

[7] Richard Hall, *The High Price of Principles* (London: Hodder and Stoughton, 1969), 169.
[8] *Ibid.*, 168.

obvious to everyone, but that did not mean that the UN system could suddenly manufacture new results for Zambia. Indeed, the very potential for development represented by copper production meant that the UN system had probably given Zambia a lower priority for aid than Tanzania.

Nevertheless, a greater influence on the part of the UN system, which was after all evident in Zambia in the form of a Regional Representative and a UN Economic Commission for Africa branch office, might have been expected. Ivan Smith's conception of his work as Personal Representative of the Secretary-General tended toward such a role. But he had left Zambia shortly before UDI to take up a temporary university appointment, and his successor, Richard Symonds, viewed the potential of the Regional Representative's position in more strictly economic terms. Ivan Smith returned to the three countries shortly after UDI on behalf of the Secretary-General, but little in the way of more concrete aid resulted. Rather, the expanded advisory and Special Fund programs, plus some IBRD assistance for road improvement, appeared to touch the limits of the capacity of the system to respond to the emergency. The response was active, direct, and planned; it was never so striking as to make a permanent platform for continuing influence on the most important decisions and policies of the government. Indeed, as it became apparent that Zambia's needs, with respect to the disruptions to its development caused by the UN program of sanctions and to the threat to its security, far outstripped any assistance that the United Nations and its sister organizations could manage, the government tended to pay less attention to the multilateral agencies on its territory.

141

MEANS OF INFLUENCE

Each of the cases described here had its particular features, and the varying means of influence that operate in the relationship between international organizations and governments receiving aid becomes visible in various degrees and with different effects.[9] These means, which depend among other factors on international practice and law, bureaucratic organization, competition for resources among governments and bureaucracies, personal roles and prestige can now be put into rough categories or types. The following paragraphs constitute an attempt to classify them.

Government Level

When governments and international organizations, using authorized persons as their representatives, come to definite understandings about their interdependent activities, the process of influence may be said to take place at the government level. The agreement to undertake the Lower Shire Valley survey is an example of action decided upon at the government level (although part of the creation of the project took place at the ministerial level, discussed below).

The most prevalent means of influence at this level appears to be *cooperative advantage*, the familiar agreement based on diplomatic negotiations that have a bargaining character. Representatives of the government and of the international agencies attempt to define the basis of activities that will as far as possible satisfy the stated or implied needs of both parties. The conditions of granting and receiving aid, developed

---

[9] Some conclusions about the limits and effects of influence are drawn in the following chapter.

through formal guidelines and bureaucratic interpretations on both sides, mark the outside limits of the negotiations; any proposal that goes much beyond these limits makes impossible any cooperative advantage and influence. When cooperative advantage can be defined and accepted, governments obtain the benefits of international aid and the organizations involved can carry out their programs.

Administrative skill often is a primary element in securing cooperative advantage. In the observed cases, the ability to penetrate the complexity of the international administrative system and to stimulate responses from it often had an important effect on government-agency relationships. Administrative skill was always necessary in formulating proposals and procedures that would be acceptable to all organizations concerned, including the recipient government. In the Wami-Pangani survey, for example, Ivan Smith's skill, tact, and persistence in using bureaucratic channels had a determining effect in reestablishing smooth relations between Tanzania and the UNDP. And in the response to UDI, the quick reassignment of UNDP advisers by means of international bureaucratic decisions probably had a favorable effect on relations between Zambia, which benefited, and the UN system. On the government side, the ability to select possible donors and to estimate likely responses had an influential effect on the international agencies. So did the ability to make rapid decisions that could actually be carried out. In this respect, the perennial lack of competent manpower and the pressure on able officials and politicians probably resulted in a reduction of potential influence by the governments on the international agencies.

It is in the nature of international institutions to represent wider interests than those defined at the government level. Programs within individual countries supposedly relate to worldwide goals and conform to a general standard to which all members accede. Therefore the *representation of wider interests* and the formulation of those interests could create situations involving influence. Underlying the influence from this source would be the review of field operations in the light of generalized doctrine regarding the goals of international organizations and also reciprocal persuasion on the part of international personnel and government representatives. Ivan Smith's unusual mandate to represent the UN Secretary-General demonstrated the relevance of wider interests in field operations and also showed how the broad range of interests on the part of international agencies can be focused on a member government. As for influence directed from governments to international agencies, the complaint by the Tanzanian Minister of Agriculture about the alleged unresponsiveness of the UNDP and Prime Minister Banda's resistance to advice from the FAO suggest that governments have means to influence the more general definitions of international goals.

The participation of many governments in the deliberative process of international institutions results in *general policy recommendations.* It is conventionally assumed that if a government representative approves a recommendation at an international meeting, his government will take the matter seriously. This outcome derives from the assumption that delegates have instructions from their governments. Therefore, if a government receiving international aid digested the results of its experience and codified its requirements, it could instruct its representatives to international deliberative bodies in such a way as to increase its influence on the general policy recommendations sent to all governments. Such recommendations are always passed along to member governments. If a government and, especially, its bureaucracies which deal with technical issues in relation to general policy, react to such recommendations, then international agencies have influence. The cases dealt with above show little evidence that governments systematically analyze their experiences with international aid. Nor is there much sign of systematic handling of general policy recommendations; reactions to these apparently occur in only indirect and inscrutable ways.

Ministerial Level

An oft-remarked attribute of international organization for technical services is the creation of direct relationships between international agencies and various national ministries.[10] This attribute is contrasted with the older practice of funneling every foreign relationship through the foreign affairs ministry—a practice which is far from abandoned. The case studies above make it obvious that at the ministerial level a variety of direct relationships with international agencies does appear. These include the means of influence discussed above under the heading, "Governmental Level," but two additional forms appear which seem relevant mainly at the ministerial level.

The first of these may be called *technical competence.* This links with the primary reason for the creation of

---

[10] By ministerial level I do not mean that the exclusive competence of ministers is involved but rather that ministries, as opposed to the government or cabinet, are engaged in the activities examined here.

international technical assistance programs: the diffusion of advanced technical skills to countries lacking them. One of the simplest means of doing this requires the assignment, usually to a ministry, of an expert who has technical competence beyond that locally available. The limited method of assigning experts (supplemented by fellowships for training abroad) was expanded in the preinvestment projects developed by the UN Special Fund before the formation of the UNDP. Both methods rely on technical competence which cannot be matched in the receiving country. It follows that recommendations from an expert adviser or the report of a preinvestment project can have influence only to the degree that advice really is wanted or is based on technical competence. Such projects as the Luangwa Valley survey illustrate the use of technical competence as a means of influence. That project included both expert advisers, who developed the basis for the preinvestment survey, and the broader kind of technical assistance characteristic of preinvestment aid.

A second means of influence which appears primarily at the ministerial level may be called *bureaucratic symbiosis*. It involves the creation and filling of bureaucratic posts which have special relevance for relations with international agencies. The post of secretary-general of the UNESCO National Commission in Tanzania illustrates this means of influence, as does the post of economic adviser to the Tanzanian agricultural ministry, which was filled by the FAO mission chief. In the first instance, ideas promoted by UNESCO presumably entered ministerial channels, while in the second, the minister's thought flowed back to the FAO. A less well defined symbiotic relation arises in the coordination offices established by national governments to deal with international aid. Because the officials gain specialized knowledge of the international agencies, they can work especially closely with their international counterparts. The symbiotic relationship of national and international bureaucracies possibly extends much farther than is generally recognized in government circles. It includes training of counterpart personnel and is also directly tied to technical competence as a means of influence.

Across Levels

In reality, none of the means of influence so far identified invariably fits neatly into one level or another, although they can usually be placed mainly at the government or ministerial level. Some other means of influence, however, by their very nature tend to affect different levels simultaneously.

A frequently used means of influence across levels can be thought of as the modern international version of *deus ex machina*. It involves the intrusion into the attention of national personnel of representatives of international organizations whose prestige and roles tend to compel reactions. A "high-powered" survey mission, such as the IBRD sends out, or the arrival of a high official of an agency, e.g., a Deputy Director-General or Director-General, on a mission that includes "selling" projects, illustrates this means of influence. The government ministers and very often the head of government must receive these visitors. For their part, the touring officials usually make a point of contacting any symbiotic bureaucrats and any personnel from their own agency. These in turn usually find the visit an occasion to voice their own views in the hope of influencing operations. The resulting stir and fanfare tend to produce waves of energy throughout the government.

147

National officials are, of course, quite able to use a similar technique. Prime Minister Banda's practice of making personal decisions and announcing his views of technical aid, as he did in the negotiations on the Lower Shire Valley survey, had the character of *deus ex machina*. Furthermore, a national government can send a minister or other representative to call on agency officials at their headquarters in an attempt to produce special attention.

Personal attributes of government officials or of international servants can sometimes have similarly wide effects. The notable leadership qualities of President Kaunda and President Nyerere tended to give them automatic influence on international programs in their territories and special attention from leading figures of international agencies. Among the international personnel, Ivan Smith cultivated a wide acquaintanceship that opened opportunities for influence across channels. International organization personnel, such as Goundry in Zambia, developed a capacity for influence by means of the confidence they received from national leaders.

Beyond the National Level

The design and operation of international aid programs and their resulting relationships between national and international agencies frequently were influenced by unanticipated actors and actions outside of the purview of the three countries observed in this study. Such actors and actions usually were the subject of little reciprocal influence from the three governments. The declaration of independence and other actions by the Ian Smith government illustrate the character of this kind of influence. The depth of influence in such situations depends on the degree of interdependence in-

148

volved. For Zambia, this influence was substantial although ancillary to Smith's purposes.[11]

Similar influence can arise from decisions by national governments with regard to their willingness to support international programs. The reluctance of the United States to give additional financial support to the UN system obviously influenced its bilateral programs and therefore its relationship with the three countries studied. So, too, did Prime Minister Vorster's more conciliatory foreign policy for South Africa. Moreover it is conceivable that such decisions, taken apart from the programs studied here, could have determinative effects on the influence of international agencies.

[11] Zambia responded to Smith's UDI, of course, but this reaction remained a secondary factor in regard to Rhodesian aims, which had primarily to do with the national status of that colony.

5.

AN INTERNATIONAL
ADMINISTRATIVE INSTRUMENT

Dᴀɢ Hᴀᴍᴍᴀʀsᴋᴊöʟᴅ once said, "In the field of economic and social policy, and of guidance and assistance to the underdeveloped areas, . . . the United Nations is in the first place to be regarded as an international administrative instrument, complementing the national administrations."[1] A decade later, field observation in East and Central Africa indicated that the activities of the UN system had not changed in kind. The phrase, "an international administrative instrument," continued accurately to characterize what could be observed. It provides a base from which conclusions, related to the hypotheses and propositions of Chapter 1, can be drawn.

Although the amount of assistance available to the less developed countries had grown remarkably during the decade after Hammarskjöld's comment, it was still almost invariably dwarfed by some or even several bilateral programs. Moreover, its total size, measured by an annual expenditure for the whole world of less than $250 million, was exceeded not only by the needs but even by some of the sectoral output in the area observed. For example, the values of metals exported by

[1] Speech at the University of California, 1954, reported in Wilder Foote and Andrew Cordier, eds., *The Public Papers of the Secretaries-General* (New York: Columbia University Press, 1972), Vol. II, 300.

Zambia in 1968 amounted to more than three times the global resources of the UNDP.[2] Furthermore, after 1970, the prospect of an increase in UNDP resources did not seem promising, especially with an unenthusiastic administration in the United States. Unless the UN system had succeeded by the time of the field observation in becoming a motivating force for economic development and social change, the prospect that more abundant resources would increase its effectiveness was unlikely for the foreseeable future.

Yet it was conceivable that even without massive resources multilateral help could be the crucial margin without which no or little economic development would be possible. This hypothesis could in no respect be verified in the field, and no indications could be found that such a special case of crucial complementarity existed. On the contrary, the real question must be whether it would have made any substantial difference if the entire multilateral program had vanished overnight or never had been started. The field observations clearly show that the rate of activity intended to produce economic development would have been slower without the multilateral programs. Nevertheless, such a conclusion does not demonstrate either that the difference in rate of activity is a significant one or that any actual economic development resulted from the planning, conferring, coming and going, and reporting. As to the difference in the rate of activity, it is important to recall that in none of the three countries observed was the UNDP the largest or necessarily the most sought after purveyor of technical assistance. The IBRD, on the other hand, did provide resources which the governments at least

[2] *Yearbook of International Trade Statistics 1968* (New York: United Nations, 1970), 940.

thought significant enough to seek out with energy and to greet with long-term commitments to conditions not entirely of their own making.

Some of the projects described here, such as the Wami-Pangani survey, and others not treated, obviously had little effect on the economy they were intended to serve or on specific planning for future development. The same might be said of a number of small-scale advisory experiences which are not described here. Other projects had a problematic role in development. But stimulating economic development is no certain matter and may reflect a fortuitous hiding hand from abroad when local circumstances have combined in unpredictable ways.[3] For instance, Malawi's successful application for an IDA loan for the Lower Shire scheme, which almost certainly has resulted in greater economic output than would have been possible without outside financing, appears to have rested more on a fortunate conjunction of bureaucratic factors than on deliberate planning and searching.

In all cases, aside from the most general goal of spurring economic development, the multilateral projects were aimed at improving the quality of government programs by injecting useful advice; preparing the way for external investment, especially through loans from the IBRD; or actually securing loans from the latter. One useful index of the success of such projects would be the prominence of multilateral aid in government pronouncements on development and long-range planning. On this basis, it is obvious that some international ventures failed. But the reasons for failure or success

[3] Albert O. Hirschman, *Development Projects Observed* (Washington: Brookings Institution, 1967), Chapter 1.

cannot be easily stated. Precise measurement appears to be an even less likely possibility.

An explanation of the useful outcome of multilateral aid might be sought in the mode of institutional organization. It seems obvious that useful aid schemes have to be conceptualized so as to provide a logical relation between their design and the expected outcome. They must moreover be carried out with dedication, energy, and imagination. Otherwise the result will surely be judged a failure by those who view it in retrospect. If multilateral organizations were organized in such a way as to increase the possibility of poor conceptualization or administration, in comparison with private, small enterprises, larger corporations, or still larger bilateral programs, then an easy explanation would be possible; a guide to policy would automatically become available to governments and multilateral organizations. But it seems probable that generalizations cannot now be confirmed with regard to mode of organization and its relationship to accomplishment. The uncertainty becomes all the greater if the possibility of a considerable degree of unplanned results is granted.

If the creation of projects alone is considered, it becomes clear that the multilateral programs did encourage ventures related to development. They sometimes furnish the crucial help needed to extend local resources. Some of this help took the form of ideas, some the form of argument and persuasion, and some a financial form. In this sense, the multilateral agencies encouraged development, assuming that some of the projects actually had the desired economic effects. At the same time, the projects which were supported fell within the definitions thought desirable at the several

153

headquarters of the multilateral agencies concerned. The secretariats of the organizations, whether from headquarters or stationed in the field, screened the submitted projects according to what they believed would fit the limits within which aid was granted. The network of multilateral organizations therefore had a certain influence on government behavior by specifying explicitly or implicitly the means of gaining benefits.

This influence emerges from the Wami-Pangani experience and was at issue in the Lower Shire Valley scheme. In both of these cases, conflicts developed between the national and international administrations over the criteria which should guide aid projects. In Tanzania, the responsible minister even reacted by raising a question of principle as to who decides what a beneficial project would be; he naturally thought that a matter for the national regime. In the Lower Shire Valley scheme, not only did differences develop between the FAO and the Prime Minister but also between the former and the World Bank representatives in the field. In both cases, the issues were resolved with compromises that gave the governments much, but not quite all, of what was demanded. Such a compromise may be taken as evidence of mutual influence. In both cases, the influence extended far up and down the ladder of access, and the Wami-Pangani case gave much evidence of a mediating filter in UNDP headquarters. In contrast, the criteria applied by the Resident Representative, UNDP headquarters, and the FAO in the Luangwa Valley case coincided extremely well with the wishes of the Zambian government. The application went forward smoothly and won general acceptance with a minimum of change. Here there was coincidence of conceptualization, rather than much mutual influence (except on

154

technical details and procedures), although it could be speculated that such an experience tends to set standards applicable over the long run and therefore represents a potential for influence by the multilateral organizations which were responsible in some measure for the creation of the projects.

To speak of filters, guidelines, and principles implies the possible existence of an integrated doctrine which is applied by international civil servants at the field level. Such a doctrine would inform the governments seeking aid and enlighten the initiatives of national civil servants. It could be referred to by international civil servants in their discussions with national officials and employed to justify their recommendations and decisions. It would be evident at numerous stages in the aid process and become an important tool in the periodic reshaping of field programs. However, field observations merely strengthened scepticism about the reality of such doctrine. The field operations observed proceeded in a remarkably empirical manner and on the basis of intuition, rather than articulated policy. This is not to say that no policies existed. The IBRD representatives in the Lower Shire Valley case and the FAO representatives in the Wami-Pangani case invoked organizational policies to justify their recommendations and decisions. But no integrated statement of development aims and methods was regularly employed or cited by anyone during the period of observation.

United Nations practice furnished good reason to raise questions about the application of a development doctrine at the field level. Each year the Economic and Social Council examines a series of draft resolutions, emanating mainly from the United Nations Secretariat and from the Specialized Agencies, on economic devel-

155

opment problems.[4] It eventually adopts most of these, directing some of them to the member states, some to the General Assembly for endorsement at what is supposed to be a more prestigious level, and some of them to the secretariats. Taken together they constitute a formidable assemblage of directives and recommendations which could be regarded as official doctrine. Because of the sources of most of these resolutions and their increasingly technical content, they could be supposed to be based firmly on experience and to be intended as guides for field operations. Moreover, from time to time, the General Assembly has adopted wide-ranging programs intended to consolidate the existing economic development work and to give direction to future activities. Good examples of such programs are the two declarations of United Nations Development Decades.[5] Further recommendations on a less grand scale mirror the increasing official concern in the Economic and Social Council with the social effects of development programs.[6]

The numerous resolutions of the General Assembly and the Economic and Social Council never were cited in observable situations or documents as a reason for any field activity whatever. There were few indications, even in response to direct questions, that the govern-

[4] Compare Walter R. Sharp, *The United Nations Economic and Social Council* (New York: Columbia University Press, 1969).

[5] United Nations General Assembly Resolutions 1710 (XVI), 19 December 1961, and 2626 (XXV), 24 October 1970.

[6] Especially United Nations General Assembly Resolutions 2542, 11 December 1969, and 2681 (XXV), 11 December 1970. See also General Assembly Resolution 2136 (XXIII), 19 December 1968, and Economic and Social Council Resolution 1139 (XLI), 29 July 1966.

ment officials who dealt with development problems knew much about the doctrines expounded by the deliberative organs. None of the advisers supplied through multilateral channels discussed their work in the abstract terms necessarily used in global recommendations. Contrasting with the grandiose rhetoric of Development Decade resolutions, the concentration in the field was on specific problems and quick results, rather than on the relationships between operating projects and theoretical approaches. For example, those most closely associated with social problems were advisers on social welfare, whose work concerned community development or labor welfare and social security. They were bound to their particular projects, and no explicit attempt was made to relate their activities to any other social aspects of development programs, even if an implicit relationship existed. Furthermore, it was extremely doubtful that the social aspects—there were some—of national plans had any relationship to advice and recommendations from the UN system.

Similar comments could be made about the relationship between the doctrinal pronouncements of international organizations and the economic content of national plans during the observation period. To link what was happening on the banks of the Kafue River, say, and what was recommended in agency headquarters in New York, Geneva, or elsewhere simply was not then possible. The national bureaucracies were not equipped to make such links and showed little interest in doing so, even when officials were questioned about the idea. National planning offices concentrated on planning exercises for the countries as wholes and made little distinction between various forms of financing the projects. Furthermore, they had relatively little experience with

157

administering plans. The finance ministries did not administer the actual development work but concentrated on obtaining funds from outside sources, on foreign exchange problems, and on familiar domestic functions. The foreign offices formally remained the principal links with international organizations at the official and representational level. But they were invariably overloaded with a hundred political matters and gave only slight attention to the efforts of international bodies to promote economic and social cooperation. Only general instructions were given to delegations and permanent missions abroad, which were left largely to their own devices, unless some immediate question with pressing security or ideological overtones arose. Nor did delegations often have the benefit of what could be a highly informed briefing from the Resident Representatives and other personnel of multilateral agencies. Clearly, Zambia or Malawi must react to a resolution on economic relations with Rhodesia or South Africa, but the likely source of such a recommendation is a politically specialized organ well within the conventional purview of a foreign office. The implications for development would be handled at the national level with little reference to the international policies in the background.

Planning offices and finance ministries generally had no shortage of advice about the manner in which they ought to proceed. In the three countries observed, the Commonwealth connection was a primary source of economists and planners. Additional advice came from missions of the IBRD, sometimes from the IMF, from the Economic Commission for Africa, and from some private agencies, such as the Ford Foundation, which have field services. Some advisers, often of high rank, were furnished by the international agencies, but their influence appeared neither to have predominated nor to have produced a working theoretical framework. Indeed, much of their work appears to have been technical, rather than conceptual, in character. Economic advisers to the governments, such as Baldwin and Goundry, did try deliberately to inject a certain degree of conceptualization into their communications with the national authorities. Because they operated at or close to the decision-making level, their influence was both more obvious and more direct than that of an adviser engaged, say, in improving the statistical service in Tanzania. Yet it would be incorrect to claim that their advice represented the injection of international organization doctrine into national government operations. They were never in such close touch with the international organizations as to represent their views, nor would their OPEX status have encouraged them to try to do so.

However, in one field, public health, field representatives of the WHO appeared to advise on the basis of recommendations made in deliberative organs at the regional and global level. In several respects, the two WHO representatives had a position that differed significantly from those of other agencies. They were accepted in all three countries as the resident senior advisers to the ministries of health. The advisers, one of whom also dealt with Malawi, were themselves trained medical practitioners, thus possessing a skill that was in short supply. They were on extended assignments, not on technical assistance missions of short duration. They were financed directly by the WHO, without the need to create a special project, but they were able in some instances to help with additional advisers directly through the WHO regular program. The results of

WHO advice could usually be seen quickly and without the necessity of difficult interpretation through economic analysis. While no sweeping changes in public health practices were made during the observation period, the advice of the WHO representatives was sought for other technical assistance projects and produced some alterations or additional provisions in some of them, especially when broad-scale planning for habitation was involved.

Aside from WHO and IBRD representatives, the UNDP Resident Representatives and their staffs most directly spoke for the whole gamut of organizations in the UN system. To them were also attached representatives of some of the specialized agencies, e.g., the FAO. They also headed the collection of subsidiary UN organizations, e.g., the WFP. The governments in fact and in law regarded the Resident Representatives as the senior delegates of the UN system. It might be thought then that the Resident Representatives would serve as active sources of the doctrines approved by international agencies as applicable to the very tasks in which the field establishment was engaged. These doctrines, it could be speculated, would become part of the thought pattern of the national government officials, in part simply by filling a vacuum, and in part by meeting the needs of national development programs.

If the Resident Representatives were to function as sources of doctrine, they would have either to perceive a vacuum of thought or to establish the relevance of their views in relation to the intentions of government planning and finance bureaus. To some extent the vacuum did exist immediately before and after independence in the three countries. Most of the senior colonial officials were on their way out, as a result of government policies or their own wishes. Their ideas, which had prevailed during the colonial period, needed revision and replacement in an era which shifted priorities away from the maintenance of law and order to economic development and political integration. All of the new governments, furthermore, were well disposed in principle to advice and help from the UN system. They had already had some experience with the benefits from that system and in working with the Resident Representatives.

The Resident Representatives, then, found themselves in a time of opportunity for their organizations. If the concepts they put before governments had relevance to perceived needs and to unfolding practices, they might be the bearers of new, integrated doctrines of state behavior and commitment. On the whole, however, the main concepts which guided the Resident Representatives related to the management of the complex administrative structures to which they belonged and to the practices of international civil services with regard to the actions of member governments. They relied primarily on the ideas of neutrality, service, and circumspection which two generations of international civil servants had elaborated for relations with member governments. However, none of the Resident Representatives and only a very few of the younger officials in their offices—the total group never exceeded twenty-five during the entire observation time—possessed the skills of trained economists. They did not lack some knowledge and sympathy with the theories of economic development which underlay some of the resolutions of the Economic and Social Council and the advice of some of the experts they helped to recruit. That did not mean, however, that the Resident Representatives were generally willing to interpret doctrinal pronouncements by UN organs for use in local conditions. During the observation period, the discussion in the Governing Council of the UNDP, it is probably fair to say, contributed little in the way of explicit doctrine. The emphasis there was more likely to fall on the pattern of distribution of projects than on the theoretical connections among them. Over time, the decisions of the Governing Council did constitute a kind of operational code. Because most of these decisions owed more to the recommendations of the UNDP headquarters staff than to anything else, it could be said that the Governing Council simply codified existing practices. Thus, UNDP doctrine remained largely implicit. More recently, the Council has been enlarged and given a stronger deliberative tone, suggesting that the situation during the observation period may have changed. Nor were statements by the Economic Commission for Africa much more applicable to local situations, for no detailed reports on national government policies were made. While the ECA could furnish some consultants, those came for defined tasks only, not for the benefit of Resident Representatives trying to fashion the pattern of multilateral aid in their jurisdictions with the tools of the economist.[7]

All three of the Resident Representatives' offices were opened under George Ivan Smith's direction, or he was in charge at the moment of independence. He clearly chose a highly cooperative, service attitude toward the local government. His policy conformed closely to a straight-forward interpretation of Hammarskjöld's doc-

[7] In this connection, see Richard Symonds, ed., *International Targets for Development* (London: Faber & Faber, 1970), especially the introduction.

trine of complementarity. It also fitted with the customary practice of the international civil service. Although the situations which arose contained novel elements for the work of international civil servants, this
doctrine enabled them to deal with much of the unexpected. Ivan Smith's contemporaries and successors—
Adu and McKitterick in Dar es Salaam, Symonds and
Gilpin in Zambia and, placed at one side, Satrap and
Menzies in Malawi—understood the byways of complex
international organizations and had had much administrative experience, sometimes in national as well as
international bureaucracies. In general, they also followed the line of complementarity but with individual
variations. It is not denegration of their work to point
out that this approach to the local governments tended
to obviate attempts to develop local policies which
would mirror general pronouncements on development
from the top of the UN system. The requests and sensitivities of the recipient governments had greater po-
tency than did any doctrinal explications from the
Resident Representatives. Consequently, in all three
countries the programs of multilateral aid from the UN
system had a fragmented appearance. The special approach of the IBRD guaranteed that its contributions
would also appear as bits and pieces, related to parts
of the local plan, but even more closely defined. No
one could confidently say that the outcome would
have been much different had other approaches been
employed. All the recipient governments showed much
sensitivity to influence from outside and thought the
multilateral aid pattern more acceptable than others
because of the neutral stance they attributed to the
donors. In addition, the resources available to the international agencies remained limited, even in the face

of such an emergency as UDI in Rhodesia created for Zambia. It remains questionable whether the resources of the international agencies ever even approached the magnitude which by itself would have assured them of a major influence on local scenes.

Once the excitement of opening new offices and establishing relations with whole new elites had been accomplished, the Resident Representatives displayed increasing sensitivity to the unpatterned collections of projects which had been secured through their offices. Some of them spoke of attempting to set their own priorities on requests from the governments and of trying to impose some pattern on the work under their direction. Others emphasized cooperation with other donors to align multilateral efforts more closely with bilateral and private aid. But the same constraints which produced fragmentation in the first place remained in effect. The government officials dealing with aid knew increasingly when and how much they could get from the multilateral donors. National political leaders remained sensitive to outside influences. The bilateral donors also had national policies and decision-makers to deal with, their programs also had various limitations and anything but full flexibility.

Furthermore, as local programs developed, the Resident Representatives and their junior staffs tended to spend more and more time on the workings of the UN system: this implied that the Resident Representative would have a wider symbolic and practical role. In the case of UNDP projects, as has been seen in the cases studied above, the Resident Representative must deal with complex autonomous organizations. Yet he must persuade them and relay their own persuasion to the governments. Sometimes he has to intervene in the internal politics of specialized agencies to find solutions satisfactory to donor governments. Aside from persuasion and skill in manipulating bureaucracies, the Resident Representative is equipped with only one major weapon: he can threaten to or actually withhold his recommendation from a plan intended to be forwarded to UNDP headquarters for eventual funding. This is almost too potent a weapon for any but extreme cases; it easily arouses resistance on the part of governments and agencies defensive of their independence.

The continuing operations of multilateral programs tended to involve additional agencies. For example, promotion of tourism and trade requires more air travel, which in turn demands good aviation facilities. These requirements created a demand for aviation advisers, who are in some instances provided through the International Civil Aviation Organization (ICAO). They need meteorological assistance, bringing about an interest in advice from the World Meteorological Organization (WMO). Such growth must have suitable management, indicating a role for the management training program of the ILO, not to speak of its vocational training program. As each one of these concentric circles of agency involvement is drawn, the complexity of the relations maintained by the Resident Representative increases. He must give expert bureaucratic advice to the local government on how to manage the increasingly involved decision-making and must himself be able to treat with the various agency headquarters, including the UNDP.

The specialized agencies used the facilities of the Resident Representatives' offices in various ways, ranging from minor bookkeeping to full representation. The activities of the Resident Representatives therefore

165

were related to the number of agencies having or promoting projects within their jurisdictions. In some cases, the specialized agency personnel deliberately urged projects on the national governments with the full knowledge that if they were requested, only the UNDP could support them. This kind of promotion helped to maintain the bureaucratic establishments within the agencies, which had been expanded in order to offer services based on UNDP contracts; it was also a means of creating new expansion. This "selling" procedure usually went on without advice from the Resident Representative, who might get wind of it informally. In any case, the agencies did not automatically defer to the Resident Representative, and their "traveling salesmen" had their own briefs, which might coincidentally fit with the Resident Representative's ideas. This created yet more complexity.

Thus, the Resident Representatives had real incentives within the UNDP framework to concentrate on administrative problems if anything but confusion were to result. They could scarcely put full attention on the development of analytical techniques, the application of existing doctrine, and the creation of new and better theoretical approaches to development needs, or even to the sharpening of perception of those needs.

The operations of the IBRD produced yet another complication with respect to multilateral development assistance. The IBRD had no formal connection at the field level with the Resident Representative. The latter did not represent the IBRD in any form, and the World Bank did not depend on the UNDP for financial support, even if it theoretically could be named as contractor for UNDP projects.[8] The IBRD had, in short, its

[8] This later occurred in UNDP projects.

own channels for dealing with governments, gathering information, and exerting influence. Yet much of the UNDP's operation was justified on the grounds that it would eventually become a basis for investment. Because the most active and sizable economic units in East and Central Africa during the observation period were the governments themselves, the World Bank, and not some arrangement in the private capital market, had to be looked upon as the most likely source of aid for the foreign exchange component of development. Therefore, it was important for both the UN system and the governments to have close and cooperative relations with the IBRD.

During the observation period, relations between the Resident Representative and the IBRD were only sporadic, although apparently characterized by less mistrust than experienced international officials had encountered elsewhere. The relationship became increasingly close later. Nevertheless, as the Lower Shire Valley case indicates, the World Bank had a reputation and prestige of its own. The proximity of important loans, which is suggested by the whole purpose of the Bank, even when it is providing nothing more than technical assistance, as in the case of its agricultural development services, attracts the interest of national policy makers. Its channel into the core of government decision-making is through the finance ministries, which necessarily have wide surveillance over whole national administrations. As a result, the World Bank, only peripherally a part of the UN system during the observation period, could at times become the leading influence in decisions on technical assistance. From the point of view of the Resident Representatives, this influence could only seem a confusion that needed to be

167

cleared up with closer cooperation and planning. The IBRD's main doctrines were still based on banking considerations, such as ability to repay and to account for expenditures. At the same time, it had moved some distance from its earlier caution about general development support for less developed countries. Nevertheless, its new sympathies had not developed so far that its officials tended enthusiastically to embrace ideas that did not have at least some clear relationships to "bankability." Later, Robert McNamara's leadership of the IBRD and the outlook on which the IDA had been based combined to make the Bank an increasingly important agency for the three countries.

SOME PERSONAL ELEMENTS

The picture of multilateral aid sketched here diverges in many respects from the model of a rational bureaucratic structure. One of the main differences can be found in the great importance of individual persons in the decision-making process. This contrasts with the model of reasonable, disciplined, rather gray bureaucrats set in a hierarchy, numerous enough to replace each other without much friction.

The number of people involved in effective decision-making[9] is remarkably small and yet always changing. This situation begins on the national government side,

[9] By effective decision-making I mean having access to proposals at an early enough stage to add or remove details at low cost to both the prospective recipients and donors; or having direct supervisory authority at several stages of the project, rather than merely at the beginning and at the end. This definition places the UNDP Governing Council, as it functioned during the observation period, outside of the effective decision-makers, except on the most unusual occasions.

168

where the chronic shortage of trained, energetic officials is the primary reason for seeking technical assistance. This shortage has every sort of recognition at the international level—ceremonial, formal, legal, informal, legislative, and administrative. It is part of the accepted doctrine of contemporary international organization. Even a casual observer in East and Central Africa would find little reason to contradict this belief. It accounted for the presence of hundreds of expatriate civil servants and technical aides, drawn not only from colonial services and from international organizations but also directly on contract and through foundations and other private groups. These expatriates were an anachronism in a time of new regimes, but they were thought necessary to the functioning of public administrations, research institutes, universities, parastatal businesses, and other organizations. Most of them in one way or another were supposed to train counterparts in order to build up national manpower resources, but given the degree of need and the slender educational basis, along with the pace of development activity, the expatriates would need considerable time to work themselves out of their jobs.

Despite the injection of foreign personnel into the countries observed, the effective decision-makers on multilateral aid within the national governments remained a very small group. Sometimes only three or four officials and politicians might be involved, sometimes perhaps as many as five times that number. Of the decision-makers involved in multilateral assistance projects, only a small proportion ever had specialized experience and duties that were clearly relevant. Most often, these were officials in the designated contact bureau for the multilateral organizations. In each of the

169

three countries studied, these never numbered more than about six to ten any one time. Frequently, they had other duties, and almost all worked under considerable pressure.

On the international side, the representation in the countries observed contained not more than three effective decision-makers per project in any of the Resident Representatives' offices. To this might be added a specialized agency representative or two for certain requests. Other international personnel were actively engaged in advisory or research functions and only informally consulted, if at all. The Resident Representatives dealt indirectly with a wider circle of officials in UNDP and specialized agency headquarters, but even there the numbers for any one project probably never exceeded ten, only one or two of whom had direct contact with the field representatives.

Although the small size of the decision-making universe in no sense implies that wrong decisions were made or that leadership or energy were defective, it does mean that individuals had great importance. If the decision-makers were regarded as cogs in a machine, each of them tended to be a major gear whose movements affected the entire operation. Furthermore, they had marked individual characteristics and came from diverse social and educational backgrounds, so that it was more difficult to substitute them one for the other than might be the case in an old, established national civil service on the European model. The international civil servants were by definition from diverse national backgrounds, including Africans, Asians, Europeans, and North and South Americans.

It follows then that the replacement of one of these officials because of retirement, reassignment, or resignation could have a sharp effect throughout the entire local multilateral aid mechanism. This was especially true of the replacement of a Resident Representative or a top-ranking aid director in the national government. Such effects were easily observed: when, for example, Menzies took over as Resident Representative from Satrap, representation received less emphasis and the creation of an integrated project list much more. Ivan Smith's inclination to give much energy to quasi-diplomatic work was followed by Adu's and Symond's much more concentrated attention on administrative efficiency and tight organization of requests. Such officials also had considerable prestige and a high rank within their own organizations. Their individual views had to be given considerable weight in their respective headquarters, and they could not be given orders without consultation, as might be the case with junior officials in a hierarchy. Thus, the entire multilateral field operation was everywhere influenced strongly by the views of the handful of officials in a decision-making capacity.

Given the indifferent force of development doctrine on actual operations and the high prestige of the leading field officials, as well as that of their opposite numbers in national governments, the potential existed for the creation of a free-wheeling field program that would justify its decisions nominally on the grounds of central policy but would in fact either serve as a tool of the national governments receiving aid or would value above other goals the participation and cooperation of others in a small group. Observations in the three countries do not support claims that such a situation existed. But the very structure of the multilateral agency-national government relationship, in a situation of low economic development, great needs, pressure on

171

manpower, and lack of national experience, suggested that such tendencies were present, although in less than critical measures.

Tendencies toward mutual cooperation and accommodation constantly were upset by the frequent transfers of personnel of both the national and international staffs. Resident Representatives rarely stay more than four years in any post; Gilpin was an exception in this regard. Junior personnel were transferred just as frequently, while technical assistance advisers usually were on year-to-year assignments and worked for international agencies that make a policy of shifting personnel. This policy probably was almost always wise, especially if the adviser had to give advice on controversial matters. Personnel attached to Special Fund projects had the longest assignments but also those with the least general policy implications. The national governments sometimes shifted personnel with startling rapidity. This was especially true within the senior ranks in Zambia, where the government strove to give its meager high-level staff broad experience and little chance to acquire vested interests and where opportunities for promotion were abundantly available.

The general impression left by this situation of free-wheeling tendencies, unsettled administrative doctrine, the small number of decision-makers with great importance of personal characteristics, and rapid turnover of personnel, was one of constant reconstruction of lines of personal and organizational contact. The situation was so fluid that whole projects lost their anchors and drifted away into indifference and abandonment. Others carried on solidly when circumstances, such as strong interest by a political figure in the government or good leading personnel and preliminary staff work, permitted.

But the unstable situation also tended to endanger past accomplishments and threaten future performance, even while it made a triumph of decentralization over any centralized control or influence in the multilateral agencies. A distant chance remained that international officials, acting with few constraints from their headquarters, could establish an overweening personal influence in the governments to which they were accredited, but it was only one of several possible outcomes of a complex process.

MICRO-LEVEL AND MACRO-THEORY

Although the primary purpose of the observation undertaken in East and Central Africa had to do with the practical operation of the multilateral aid system, the data uncovered relate closely to other, more theoretical approaches to understanding international organization. Without pretending to a definitive statement, certain conclusions can be drawn on which further research may be based.

The observed behavior of national officials and politicians was directed primarily toward obtaining multilateral aid for defined projects. Whether the ideas for such projects originated in their own ranks or were brought to them from outside, often through international officials, made little difference in their actions. They sought support for what they understood as economic development in national terms. Their aims, according to their statements and objections to multilateral agency conditions, had little or nothing overtly to do with the construction of a particular world order or with the fostering of a system of international organization.

The only possible observed exception to this generalization grew out of the Zambian government's reaction to UDI in Rhodesia. Zambian antipathy toward the racist tendencies of the Ian Smith government and toward its denial of majority rights fitted into a widely accepted framework of international goals. Yet economic development of Zambia was not generally perceived by officials and politicians as a means of eliminating the objectionable policies of the governments in southern Africa. Rather, this was a goal set by Zambia for its own people. The racist policies of South Africa and Rhodesia and the colonial government of the Portuguese territories interfered with these development goals. Zambia profited briefly by taking over some of the development projects that had been created for Rhodesia, but when the major goal of building a railroad to Dar es Salaam failed to received practical backing from the IBRD, the Zambian government gave no thought to abandoning it on the grounds that it would not fit a pattern approved and supported by the international agencies. Along with Tanzania, it eventually found help from the People's Republic of China and received much less impressive aid from international agencies. Meanwhile, the Malawi government chose a less hostile response to UDI but found no consequent reduction of interest by the international agencies. Indeed the IBRD was able to finance major projects in Malawi.

Although the consequences of their general policies toward South Africa, Rhodesia, and Portugal undoubtedly influenced the development programs in Zambia and Malawi and to a perhaps lesser extent in Tanzania, it remains unclear how much attention the governments

174

gave to their relations with the multilateral aid agencies in this regard. But this consideration affects the task of organizing international relations. It might be understood better through additional research, especially if it were possible to explore the nature of government discussions and perceptions of the relationships between aid and high politics and to determine the attitudes of leading decision-makers.

Similarly, at the level of the office of Resident Representative, little evidence exists of decisions deliberately designed to aid in the creation of a system of international organization, except insofar as the functioning of existing institutions automatically tended in that direction. The primary task was to organize requests for aid, put them in good form, and shepherd them through the long process of obtaining financial support and bringing international personnel to the job. This was primarily administrative work and was recognized as such by the Resident Representatives, who usually deemphasized their role in a vast network of institutions intended to foster international peace as well as welfare. In this regard, the political tasks of Ivan Smith stood out as an exception. His work did not result in institutionalization of systematic political relationships nor in the observable creation of doctrines to guide governments and international officials. Seen from the field, the usual pattern of relationships at higher headquarters was consistent with the views in the Resident Representatives' offices. The agency personnel simply proceeded with their work of running their organizations and trying to extend and improve what they did.

This raises the question as to whether the complex interrelationships among organizations and their personnel might be understood on the basis of sociological research on organizations.[10] A large body of theory and empirical research into organizational behavior exists. Some of it might be applied in field research on international organization. It might, for example, be used to sketch an environment of organizations interacting with each other, setting goals, maintaining themselves, competing with each other, and defending themselves from attack. Such an approach would emphasize the rearrangement of functions within organizations as new challenges appear and would trace the patterns of accommodation and conflict among organizations, including those within the national government. Such description and analysis might lead to answers about the relative importance given to economic aid plans and considerations of national security in making policy decisions and in ordering functions and structures within international organizations and within national regimes.

The economic development activities dealt with here form an important basis for Functionalist and Neofunctionalist theories of international organization. The Functionalists maintain that a separation of technical from political functions is possible and necessary to the growth of cooperation across national borders. The more sophisticated Neo-functionalist approach seeks evidence of integration among government and elites as the result of deliberate policies of cooperation and political decisions promoted through international institu-

[10] Haas, *Beyond the Nation State*, and Cox and Jacobson, *Anatomy of Influence*, discuss organization theory and its uses in research on international organization. According to Charles Perrow, *Complex Organizations* (Glenview, Ill.: Scott, Foresman & Co., 1972), 14, "organizations are tools for shaping the world as one wishes it to be shaped."

tions. Both sorts of theory raise questions about the significance of the kind of activity observed in East and Central Africa.

It would distort the findings of the field observation to fit them neatly into one or the other approach. But it seems clear that economic aid activities were not undertaken either with the intention of keeping them separate from some vague category labeled political or with the hope of producing integration. Rather, the national state may tend to grow in strength through the sorts of projects undertaken in East and Central Africa with multilateral help.[11] If economic development is spurred, then presumably governments can reward their peoples for their support or can mobilize them more efficiently. Moreover, if politics is viewed as a process of making authoritative divisions of scarce rewards, the development projects have a direct relationship. Nevertheless, awareness of possible long-term international effects on the part of decision-makers involved with multilateral aid appeared to be limited or implicit. Most decisions involved relatively short-term problems, such as how to design a request so as to get maximum return. If a long-term element is involved in such proceedings, it remained in the background. On no occasion was there explicit recognition of the possibility that a particular project might produce some integrative effect. This was true even in those East African regional projects in which Tanzania participated; their overriding goal was to obtain a benefit for the country, even if it had to be shared with others. No choice to foster regional projects deliberately for the sake of encouraging integration appeared to come into play.

[11] Haas, *Beyond the Nation State*, 494.

It could be argued that the nature of economic development, especially that requiring multilateral aid, tended to raise the level of international cooperation and decision-making. This argument, familiar in Functionalist discussions, implies a learning process within the governments and seems to assume that international officials have already accomplished their learning tasks. The argument also implies an interdependency of economic systems. Field observations do not immediately sustain this argument. The lack of any integrated doctrine about economic development and the role of international institutions in that process leads to the conclusion that any learning was slow and fragmented indeed, because no framework really existed. The lessons that could be drawn from experience with international aid could not be formulated, except in an empirical, short-term fashion; few governments or institutions possessed the analytical equipment to learn in this deliberate way. Thus, neither the doctrine produced by international organizations nor the ideas that could be formulated on the basis of experience appear to have been made part of national government institutions or to have played a visible part in the relations at the field level between governments and international organizations.

Unless the learning process is built into bureaucratic practice, it affects only individuals. Clearly, national officials and politicians who attended international meetings returned with knowledge of the possibilities offered through multilateral aid. Training programs in some instances had similar results. But the turbulence of national administrations, the rapid turnover of personnel, and the pressure on competent officials all took their toll. It often appeared that only a lucky chance

178

brought a senior official with notions about multilateral aid to the proper place at the proper time. That it did happen tends to support the Neo-functionalist faith that a learning process takes place by fits and starts as the result of field programs. At the same time, knowledge about such incidents remains fragmentary; they occur, but not enough observation and data are available to understand their rate and significance for the formation of doctrine for governments.

The international officials in the Resident Representatives' offices might be looked to as the repositories of learning about the theory of multilateral aid. Yet the constraints imposed by their general disinterest in doctrinal questions and their approach as international civil servants prevented this possibility from developing into a very strong force. The ever present possibility of cross-pressures from governments and international agencies also tended to inhibit the formation of doctrinal statements. Furthermore, the constant transferring of personnel tended to reduce the memory effect. Even if an effective start on a learning process could be made, a single transfer might have so great an impact within the small group of decision-makers that little of the effect of the lessons would remain. Nevertheless, this aspect of the learning process may be more subtle and pervasive than could be observed. Further observation over a longer period, using carefully designed measurements, might provide positive indications.

During the observation period, it was evident that learning about the techniques of manipulating international organizations for the purpose of obtaining aid took place. At an uneven pace, increasing numbers of national officials and politicians came into contact with multilateral aid. The experience created a diffuse memory of how to cope with practical problems. This memory was present in an increasing number of ministries as the result of transfers of personnel and the widening variety of projects over the years. The international personnel charged with relations with the governments invariably specialized in bringing forth responses from the complex system of organizations. Those international personnel primarily concerned with substantive technical assistance tasks also frequently knew a good deal about their organizations. The two groups possessed a memory of techniques, and it usually was in their interest to advance their art as rapidly as possible. They learned by doing and communicated the results in some degree to national government personnel, especially at the point of contact with aid coordinating agencies.

Whether a habit of international cooperation—the cherished "spill-over" effect of the Functionalist theorists —emerged from the experience of manipulating international organizations remains doubtful. Field observation failed to show a steady broadening of interest in applying for aid from multilateral organizations. Rather, there were a number of indications that national officials were beginning to form their own ideas of which requests should be sent to multinational agencies and which to bilateral or private donors. Requests were more often made with an eye to the donor most likely to respond favorably in the shortest possible time. National officials increasingly became aware of the limitations, caused by restricted resources or by policy preferences, of the several multilateral donors. In this respect, the international officials taught their counterparts what they might expect. Such perceptions of limitations accord ill with the expectation on the part of Functionalist theorists that successful technical cooper-

180

ation in one area tends to spread to others. It points rather to an encapsulation of aid programs within limits determined by vague policy prescriptions and much more precise administrative interpretations. If multilateral aid programs are to grow into a network of interdependence, the existing patterns of operations analyzed here must be broken up and reformed as the result of some outside stimulus.

The field operations observed during this study could perhaps also be further treated within the framework of transnational politics.[12] If the multilateral aid groups were seen as transnational bodies—existing under international control, using personnel of several nationalities, and operating within national territories—they could be analyzed for their effects on the nature of the states in which they worked. During the time of observation, however, the ability of national governments to manipulate international organizations seems to have grown. If at a later stage the transnational bodies were to exercise a new influence, additional observation would disclose it. At that time, it would also be appropriate to raise the question of whether a growing transnational elite of expert administrators, experienced at running their complex machines, could be brought under more general and effective direction with regard to goals and the way their work promoted them.

It is easy to conjure up a vision of numbers of skillful officials keeping their organizations going and providing themselves with work, whether or not it had any rele-

[12] See Joseph S. Nye, Jr., and Robert O. Keohane, "Transnational Relations and World Politics," *International Organization*, XXV, 4 (Autumn 1971), 797–801; and Samuel H. Huntington, "Transnational Organizations in World Politics," *World Politics*, XXV, 3 (April 1973), 333–68.

vance to the people who were expected to benefit. This vision of an uncontrolled international bureaucracy perhaps is far-fetched, but, given the present discontinuity between declared policy and field operations, it remains a possibility which indeed may have been realized in other settings.[13] The influence of the multilateral aid agencies and their projects on the recipient governments observed, however, was limited. It was also particular, relating far more to practical operations than to prescribed goals. The machinery of the relationship functioned to bring aid for development projects, whether or not these made a complete pattern. On the whole, the influence of the UN system on international security policy had little connection with the success or failure of the economic aid system. Yet an organizational symbiosis appeared to be developing. If its roots are fed with the necessary support from rich donor countries, it could grow more and produce as yet unknown forms.

[13] Compare Hayter, *Aid as Imperialism*, and Nairn, *International Aid to Thailand*, Chapter 11; and Karl Kaiser, "Transnational Relations as a Threat to the Democratic Process," *International Organization*, XXV, 3 (Summer 1971), 713–15.

INDEX

Books Written under the Auspices of the Center of International Studies
PRINCETON UNIVERSITY

Gabriel A. Almond, *The Appeals of Communism* (Princeton University Press 1954)

William W. Kaufmann, ed., *Military Policy and National Security* (Princeton University Press 1956)

Klaus Knorr, *The War Potential of Nations* (Princeton University Press 1956)

Lucian W. Pye, *Guerrilla Communism in Malaya* (Princeton University Press 1956)

Charles De Visscher, *Theory and Reality in Public International Law*, trans. by P. E. Corbett (Princeton University Press 1957; rev. ed. 1968)

Bernard C. Cohen, *The Political Process and Foreign Policy: The Making of the Japanese Peace Settlement* (Princeton University Press 1957)

Myron Weiner, *Party Politics in India: The Development of a Multi-Party System* (Princeton University Press 1957)

Percy E. Corbett, *Law in Diplomacy* (Princeton University Press 1959)

Rolf Sannwald and Jacques Stohler, *Economic Integration: Theoretical Assumptions and Consequences of European Unification*, trans. by Herman Karreman (Princeton University Press 1959)

Klaus Knorr, ed., *NATO and American Security* (Princeton University Press 1959)

Gabriel A. Almond and James S. Coleman, eds., *The Politics of the Developing Areas* (Princeton University Press 1960)

Herman Kahn, *On Thermonuclear War* (Princeton University Press 1960)

Sidney Verba, *Small Groups and Political Behavior: A Study of Leadership* (Princeton University Press 1961)

Robert J. C. Butow, *Tojo and the Coming of the War* (Princeton University Press 1961)

Glenn H. Snyder, *Deterrence and Defense: Toward a Theory of National Security* (Princeton University Press 1961)

Klaus Knorr and Sidney Verba, eds., *The International System: Theoretical Essays* (Princeton University Press 1961)

Peter Paret and John W. Shy, *Guerrillas in the 1960's* (Praeger 1962)

George Modelski, *A Theory of Foreign Policy* (Praeger 1962)

Klaus Knorr and Thornton Read, eds., *Limited Strategic War* (Praeger 1963)

Frederick S. Dunn, *Peace-Making and the Settlement with Japan* (Princeton University Press 1963)

Arthur L. Burns and Nina Heathcote, *Peace-Keeping by United Nations Forces* (Praeger 1963)

Richard A. Falk, *Law, Morality, and War in the Contemporary World* (Praeger 1963)

James N. Rosenau, *National Leadership and Foreign Policy: A Case Study in the Mobilization of Public Support* (Princeton University Press 1963)

Gabriel A. Almond and Sidney Verba, *The Civic Culture: Political Attitudes and Democracy in Five Nations* (Princeton University Press 1963)

Bernard C. Cohen, *The Press and Foreign Policy* (Princeton University Press 1963)

Richard L. Sklar, *Nigerian Political Parties: Power in an Emergent African Nation* (Princeton University Press 1963)

Peter Paret, *French Revolutionary Warfare from Indochina to Algeria: The Analysis of a Political and Military Doctrine* (Praeger 1964)

Harry Eckstein, ed., *Internal War: Problems and Approaches* (Free Press 1964)

Cyril E. Black and Thomas P. Thornton, eds., *Communism*

and Revolution: The Strategic Uses of Political Violence (Princeton University Press 1964)

Miriam Camps, *Britain and the European Community 1955-1963* (Princeton University Press 1964)

Thomas P. Thornton, ed., *The Third World in Soviet Perspective: Studies by Soviet Writers on the Developing Areas* (Princeton University Press 1964)

James N. Rosenau, ed., *International Aspects of Civil Strife* (Princeton University Press 1964)

Sidney I. Ploss, *Conflict and Decision-Making in Soviet Russia: A Case Study of Agricultural Policy, 1953-1963* (Princeton University Press 1965)

Richard A. Falk and Richard J. Barnet, eds., *Security in Disarmament* (Princeton University Press 1965)

Karl von Vorys, *Political Development in Pakistan* (Princeton University Press 1965)

Harold and Margaret Sprout, *The Ecological Perspective on Human Affairs, With Special Reference to International Politics* (Princeton University Press 1965)

Klaus Knorr, *On the Uses of Military Power in the Nuclear Age* (Princeton University Press 1966)

Harry Eckstein, *Division and Cohesion in Democracy: A Study of Norway* (Princeton University Press 1966)

Cyril E. Black, *The Dynamics of Modernization: A Study in Comparative History* (Harper and Row 1966)

Peter Kunstadter, ed., *Southeast Asian Tribes, Minorities, and Nations* (Princeton University Press 1967)

E. Victor Wolfenstein, *The Revolutionary Personality: Lenin, Trotsky, Gandhi* (Princeton University Press 1967)

Leon Gordenker, *The UN Secretary-General and the Maintenance of Peace* (Columbia University Press 1967)

Oran R. Young, *The Intermediaries: Third Parties in International Crises* (Princeton University Press 1967)

James N. Rosenau, ed., *Domestic Sources of Foreign Policy* (Free Press 1967)

Richard F. Hamilton, *Affluence and the French Worker in the Fourth Republic* (Princeton University Press 1967)

Linda B. Miller, *World Order and Local Disorder: The United Nations and Internal Conflicts* (Princeton University Press 1967)

Henry Bienen, *Tanzania: Party Transformation and Economic Development* (Princeton University Press 1967)

Wolfram F. Hanrieder, *West German Foreign Policy, 1949-1963: International Pressures and Domestic Response* (Stanford University Press 1967)

Richard H. Ullman, *Britain and the Russian Civil War: November 1918-February 1920* (Princeton University Press 1968)

Robert Gilpin, *France in the Age of the Scientific State* (Princeton University Press 1968)

William B. Bader, *The United States and the Spread of Nuclear Weapons* (Pegasus 1968)

Richard A. Falk, *Legal Order in a Violent World* (Princeton University Press 1968)

Cyril E. Black, Richard A. Falk, Klaus Knorr and Oran R. Young, *Neutralization and World Politics* (Princeton University Press 1968)

Oran R. Young, *The Politics of Force: Bargaining During International Crises* (Princeton University Press 1969)

Klaus Knorr and James N. Rosenau, eds., *Contending Approaches to International Politics* (Princeton University Press 1969)

James N. Rosenau, ed., *Linkage Politics: Essays on the Convergence of National and International Systems* (Free Press 1969)

John T. McAlister, Jr., *Viet Nam: The Origins of Revolution* (Knopf 1969)

Jean Edward Smith, *Germany Beyond the Wall: People, Politics and Prosperity* (Little, Brown 1969)

James Barros, *Betrayal from Within: Joseph Avenol, Secretary-General of the League of Nations, 1933-1940* (Yale University Press 1969)

Charles Hermann, *Crises in Foreign Policy: A Simulation Analysis* (Bobbs-Merrill 1969)

Robert C. Tucker, *The Marxian Revolutionary Idea: Essays on Marxist Thought and Its Impact on Radical Movements* (W. W. Norton 1969)

Harvey Waterman, *Political Change in Contemporary France: The Politics of an Industrial Democracy* (Charles E. Merrill 1969)

Cyril E. Black and Richard A. Falk, eds., *The Future of the International Legal Order. Vol. I: Trends and Patterns* (Princeton University Press 1969)

Ted Robert Gurr, *Why Men Rebel* (Princeton University Press 1969)

C. Sylvester Whitaker, *The Politics of Tradition: Continuity and Change in Northern Nigeria 1946-1966* (Princeton University Press 1970)

Richard A. Falk, *The Status of Law in International Society* (Princeton University Press 1970)

Klaus Knorr, *Military Power and Potential* (D. C. Heath 1970)

Cyril E. Black and Richard A. Falk, eds., *The Future of the International Legal Order. Vol. II: Wealth and Resources* (Princeton University Press 1970)

Leon Gordenker, ed., *The United Nations in International Politics* (Princeton University Press 1971)

Cyril E. Black and Richard A. Falk, eds., *The Future of the International Legal Order. Vol. III: Conflict Management* (Princeton University Press 1971)

Francine R. Frankel, *India's Green Revolution: Political Costs of Economic Growth* (Princeton University Press 1971)

Harold and Margaret Sprout, *Toward a Politics of the Planet Earth* (Van Nostrand Reinhold 1971)

Cyril E. Black and Richard A. Falk, eds., *The Future of the International Legal Order. Vol. IV: The Structure of the International Environment* (Princeton University Press 1972)

Gerald Garvey, *Energy, Ecology, Economy* (W. W. Norton 1972)

Richard Ullman, *The Anglo-Soviet Accord* (Princeton University Press 1973)

Klaus Knorr, *Power and Wealth: The Political Economy of International Power* (Basic Books 1973)

Anton Bebler, *Military Rule in Africa: Dahomey, Ghana, Sierra Leone, and Mali* (Praeger Publishers 1973)

Robert C. Tucker, *Stalin as Revolutionary 1879-1929: A Study in History and Personality* (W. W. Norton 1973)

Edward L. Morse, *Foreign Policy and Interdependence in Gaullist France* (Princeton University Press 1973)

Henry Bienen, *Kenya: The Politics of Participation and Control* (Princeton University Press 1974)

Gregory J. Massell, *The Surrogate Proletariat: Moslem Women and Revolutionary Strategies in Soviet Central Asia, 1919-1929* (Princeton University Press 1974)

James N. Rosenau, *Citizenship Between Elections: An Inquiry Into The Mobilizable American* (Free Press 1974)

Ervin Laszlo, *A Strategy For The Future: The Systems Approach To World Order* (Braziller 1974)

John R. Vincent, *Nonintervention and International Order* (Princeton University Press 1974)

Jan H. Kalicki, *The Pattern of Sino-American Crises: Political-Military Interactions in the 1950s* (Cambridge University Press 1975)

Klaus Knorr, *The Power of Nations: The Political Economy of International Relations* (Basic Books, Inc. 1975)

James P. Sewell, *UNESCO and World Politics: Engaging in International Relations* (Princeton University Press 1975)

Richard A. Falk, *A Global Approach to National Policy* (Harvard University Press 1975)

Harry Eckstein and Ted Robert Gurr, *Patterns of Authority: A Structural Basis for Political Inquiry* (John Wiley & Sons 1975)

Cyril E. Black, Marius B. Jansen, Herbert S. Levine, Marion J. Levy, Jr., Henry Rosovsky, Gilbert Rozman, Henry D. Smith, II, and S. Frederick Starr, *The Modernization of Japan and Russia* (Free Press 1975)

LIBRARY OF CONGRESS CATALOGING IN PUBLICATION DATA

Gordenker, Leon, 1923-
  International aid and national decisions.

  Includes index.
  1. Economic assistance.   2. United Nations—Economic
assistance.   3. International cooperation.
  I. Title.
HC60.G62   338.91   76-3257
ISBN 0-691-05662-5